Multicultural Marketing

Selling to a Diverse America

Marlene L. Rossman

American Management Association

New York • Atlanta • Boston • Chicago • Kansas City • San Francisco • Washington, D.C.
Brussels • Mexico City • Tokyo • Toronto

This publication is designed to provide accurate and authoritative information in regard to the subject matter covered. It is sold with the understanding that the publisher is not engaged in rendering legal, accounting, or other professional service. If legal advice or other expert assistance is required, the services of a competent professional person should be sought.

Library of Congress Cataloging-in-Publication Data

Rossman, Marlene L.
    Multicultural marketing : selling to a diverse America / Marlene
L. Rossman.
      p. cm.
    Inclubes bibliographical references and index.
    ISBN 0-8144-5071-7
    ISBN 0-8144-7921-9 (pbk.)
    1. Market segmentation—United States. 2. Minorities as
consumers—United States. I. Title.
HF5415.127.R673   1994
658.8'348—dc20   93-41996
                                                    CIP

Printing number

10 9 8 7 6 5 4 3

Contents

Preface

When I began working in the field of marketing and market research in the late 1970s, I was heavily involved in the emerging field of international marketing. I kept urging my clients to understand the importance of segmentation; an ad campaign that works in Puerto Rico, I found myself repeating endlessly, is not going to work in Argentina just because people speak Spanish in both countries. And what sells in Japan will not necessarily sell in Korea, even though both countries are in East Asia.

Later, as I brought my international experience back home, I realized that segmentation is just as important in the U.S. market as it is in the international market, if not more so. Although the word *multicultural* first appeared in print in 1941, until recently most U.S. businesses and advertisers continued to act as if this country were made up of nothing but traditional white families. They ignored huge—and potentially very profitable—segments of the population, including ethnics and minorities (blacks, Hispanics, Asians, Americans with disabilities, gays, and others).

Seeing marketers ignore the potential of these segments and sometimes discriminate against them reminded me, in many ways, of how I had felt as a woman doing business in male-dominated countries overseas.

In 1989 I began consulting for a large New York trade association whose member companies complained that their best salesmen couldn't close a sale to women customers. When I went into the field, I observed the male-oriented sales tactics and, worse, the unconscious discrimination commonly directed toward women. To help counter these practices, I designed and delivered ongoing sales training seminars on "Selling to Women." This situation was another example, I realized, of how mainstream marketers all too often "just don't get it."

All these ideas came together in 1991, when another of my clients, Training Management Corporation (located in New Jersey), asked me to help design and present seminars on selling to ethnic markets for a telecommunications company.

A short time later, Adrienne Hickey, senior editor at AMACOM, who had read my book *The International Businesswoman of the 1990s*, asked me to write a book on international marketing. I preferred to focus on the U.S. domestic market and counteroffered a book on marketing to ethnic segments in the United States. Given the importance of cultural diversity in America today, Adrienne jumped at the idea, and this book was born. Since that day, Adrienne has been a supportive and patient editor who has given me guidance and direction.

Another person I must thank is my tireless market research associate, Christine Jaros, who helped me in more ways than I can list—everything from pursuing and interviewing senior executives to pitching in at the computer terminal when my system went down on the eve of submitting the manuscript.*

I also owe special thanks to Dr. Diane Simpson of Simpson International, New York, for her guidance and expertise; to Julie McCormack and Jacqueline Griesback for research; to the many busy executives who so generously took the time to share their valuable experience with me, including Larry Glover, Sonia Green, Debra Sandler, Bill Orton, Chuck Morrisson, Mike Quon, Kathryn Leary, Isabel Valdes, Eleanor Yu, Dr. Gonzalo Soruco, Noel Day, George Rosenbaum, Joseph Lam, Dave Mulryan, Al Anderson, Felix Burrows, Roberto Orci, and countless others; and most of all to my husband, Elliot Silverman, to whom I dedicate this book.

So, marketers, listen up! An investment in a marketing

---

*Except where I have indicated a published source, the quotations in this book are from interviews.

campaign targeted to an ethnic or minority segment almost always produces far higher returns than a similar investment in the mainstream market. The opportunities are out there. Go out and get them!

Author's Note

Although I discuss the ethnic, religious, and lifestyle diversity of the United States, this is a marketing book. My aim is to help marketers increase profits for their companies, not to make political or social statements.

As marketers, we often have to deal with generalities—but remember that generalities are exactly that. It's important for a marketer to observe that a large percentage of one ethnic group likes Coke, while another ethnic group prefers Pepsi. Let's not forget, however, that there are probably hundreds of thousands of individuals in the first group who drink Pepsi or Dr. Pepper or apple juice.

In the same way, it's important to bear in mind that comparisons are just comparisons, not judgments. To say that one nation's culture centers around the individual, whereas another culture emphasizes the group, is not to say that one is better than the other. Different just means different.

This book is meant to be an eye-opener. America is such a diverse country, and the marketing issues resulting from that diversity are so complex, that it would take ten years and a book ten times the size of this one to cover all the relevant issues.

My hope is that this book will point you in the right direction so that you can do the research and find the best ways to target the right segment for your products and services.

With all the multicultural segments in the United States, this is one great country. And what makes it such a great country is our heritage of mutual respect and tolerance.

—MLR

Multicultural Marketing

1

America's Changing Face

America has always been a consumer's—and a marketer's—paradise. The United States is a vast market of more than 255 million people who, despite their cultural diversity, have all been influenced in one way or another by the American dream. It has always been a country of immigrants, most coming to the United States to improve their lives, some coming not at all by choice. But everyone who has come to this, the greatest of all consumerist societies, has been caught up in the goal of "getting and spending."

Compared to the ancient states of Europe, Asia, and Africa, the United States is a young country. In almost 220 years of existence, we have been looked at by others as the powerful upstart, "big (but young) brother." We have been called naive and unsophisticated, as well as by any number of unpublishable epithets. Often, one group or another in our heterogeneous society has been reviled or ignored by "pure" racial and ethnic groups, not only outside the United States but inside, as well. But the true spirit of America is the dynamism that different groups have brought here and that has become integrated into mainstream American culture.

Call Americans wasteful, materialistic, concerned only with consuming, yet we are the envy and the dream of millions of people worldwide who are hoping or fighting to get into this country.

Many come for purposes other than consuming for its own

sake; many would like to avoid starving to death or being put into jail for opposing their country's politician of the moment. Ultimately, however, all are caught up in the rows of shining goods and tantalizing services that make up the trappings of the mythical American dream.

The Diverse Market

Our job as marketers is getting a lot tougher these days. Although the United States has never had a homogeneous culture or population, until recently it was safe for companies to pretend that it did. But no longer. Because of the new groups of immigrants coming to our shores and their different patterns of assimilation, and because of the growing number of ethnic and racial minorities living in the United States, we need to track the changing trends in our population. We need to develop goods and services targeted to different groups and their individual needs.

That's not enough, however. In addition to developing new goods and services, we need to find ways to appeal to and reach many segments of our diverse population.

Some marketers are already riding this wave. Levi Strauss's Dockers slacks for men ran an ad on prime-time television that covered all the ethnic bases; it featured three handsome young men, an African-American, an Asian, and a Caucasian. Some observers thought the camaraderie among these three could also suggest that they were gay.

It might not seem surprising that Budweiser beer would run a TV ad in which a young fellow's girlfriend helps him train for a race that he then wins, after which they flirt outrageously (and suggestively) over cold beers. What is surprising about the ad, which appeared on prime-time TV in 1992, is that the woman is able-bodied and the man is in a wheelchair. Brewers have always used sex to sell beer, but never before has the idea of a sexually active athlete with disabilities been seen as attractive to middle America.

From Ozzie and Harriet to the Cosbys

If you have any doubt about the massive changes taking place in American society, just turn on the television. You'll see that over the last forty years we have moved from Ozzie and Harriet to the Cosbys, from scotch and soda to margaritas, from Walter Cronkite to Connie Chung, and from Chevrolet to Honda. Today, Jesse Jackson is an elder statesman; McDonald's sells burritos along with cheeseburgers; and Azucar Moreno, a Hispanic female pop group (whose name means brown sugar), does prime-time national television ads for Diet Coke.

During the late 1950s Campbell's Soup Company could reach half of all American households just by sponsoring "Lassie" on television. That may have been the last time things were so simple. Such a uniform market no longer exists as a result of the many changes reshaping American society.

By 1993 the networks' share of the prime-time television audience had dropped to about 70 percent from 92 percent in 1979. And even if marketers could reach everyone with one commercial, that commercial would no longer appeal to every segment of the market. Even good old Campbell's has regionalized its products and marketing mix to appeal to wildly divergent segments, such as yuppies, ethnics, the elderly, and sodium and fat watchers.

The 1980s—The Decade of Change

The U.S. government's 1990 census shows that America's population changed more rapidly in the 1980s than in any other decade of this century. Nearly one of every four Americans claims African, Asian, Hispanic, or American Indian ancestry, compared to only one in five in the 1980 census. The rate of increase in the minority population between 1980 and 1990 was nearly twice the rate of increase between 1970 and 1980.

The rate of change was even greater than these government statistics show. The Census Bureau admits that it vastly undercounted minorities; for example, it acknowledges missing one in twenty blacks and Hispanics. Even using census figures, however, the total number of minority residents was about 62 million in the early 1990s. The official census numbers indicate the presence of a little over 30 million blacks (about 12 percent of the population), 22.4 million Hispanics (about 9 percent), 7.3 million Asians (about 3 percent), and 2 million American Indians (about .8 percent).

Whites still make up more than 75 percent of the total population of the United States, according to the census, but that percentage is declining. (The Census Bureau's definition of white includes the majority of Hispanics, who can be of any race. The Bureau recognizes only four racial categories: white, black, Asian, and American Indian.) More important, the Hispanic population increased more than 50 percent between 1980 and 1990; the Asian population increased more than 107 percent.

A Nation of Minorities

If current levels of Hispanic immigration continue, according to researchers at the Urban Institute, a Washington, D.C., research firm, Hispanic residents will number 39 million by 2010, surpassing blacks as the largest minority group. The number of Asians is expected to grow to almost 22 million by 2020. Black immigrants from the Caribbean and Africa, who now number well over 1 million, will triple their numbers by 2010. If these trends continue, the United States may have no single majority racial or ethnic group by the middle of the twenty-first century.

The engine driving the increase in ethnic diversity is the relative youth of minority populations. Hispanics were the youngest overall group recorded by the 1990 census, with a median age of twenty-four years. Blacks were the second youngest, at 25.6, while races categorized as "other" (mainly Asians) had a median age of twenty-seven, and whites had a median age close to thirty-three.

The change is happening much faster in some parts of the country than in others. In the early 1980s, two thirds of

Californians were whites of European ancestry; by the turn of the century, California will have a majority of minorities.

Los Angeles already has the second largest population of Filipinos, Koreans, Mexicans, and Salvadorans of any city in the world, along with significant numbers of Chinese, Ethiopians, Indians, Indonesians, Iranians, Pacific Islanders, Druze, Tamils, and Vietnamese. Los Angeles is a supremely cosmopolitan city; its residents speak more than eighty languages and represent more than one hundred ethnic and cultural backgrounds. You can eat in a restaurant featuring a different ethnic cuisine practically every night of the year without repeating yourself.

Changing Tastes

These demographic changes are affecting everyone. When you eat an "all-American" diet of a bagel for breakfast, a slice of pizza for lunch, and a hamburger for dinner, you may not realize that all of these foods were introduced into the United States by immigrants. The impact of immigrants may be even clearer to you if you have a breakfast burrito at McDonald's, sushi for lunch, and Szechuan chicken for dinner. And if you still aren't sure about "immigrant power," you should know that in 1991, salsa outsold ketchup by $40 million in U.S. retail sales.

In 1992, total salsa sales hit $500 million—up almost 12 percent from 1991. Elizabeth Rozin, a cookbook author, explains that the mainstream palate is changing, because the mainstream itself is changing—it no longer consists exclusively of white American Protestants. And in the salty snack category, the penetration rate of tortilla chips has hit close to 60 percent of all U.S households.

Taquerias, little taco stands selling Mexican specialties, once could only be found in the Southwest and the West. Today, Mexican food has become so popular in New York that one *taqueria* is owned and staffed by a Chinese family. Packaged tortillas can be found in practically every U.S. supermarket. Similarly, producers of packaged soul food are finding tremendous interest nationally in their meals, even in upscale neighborhoods.

Diversity in the Marketplace

The trend in every aspect of American life is toward greater cultural, ethnic, and linguistic diversity. Hispanics, Asians, African-Americans, and other culturally distinct segments can't all be successfully targeted with the same goods and services via the same marketing and advertising strategies that succeeded when the United States was (or thought it was) a monolithic, Anglo-dominated market.

In these difficult economic times, businesses have learned that money is just as green when it is spent by people of color. Jack Kraft, vice chairman and CEO of Leo Burnett Company, a Chicago-based ad agency, explains that recessionary times make companies look at every market segment a little more deeply.

No longer does it suffice to dub English commercials into Spanish with lip movements out of synch or to translate print ads word for word, which can result in unintentional obscenities, as the Perdue poultry company found in 1987. (The popular ad in which company owner Frank Perdue explains that "it takes a tough man to make a tender chicken" was translated into Spanish for the East Coast market by someone not familiar with regional slang. The translation came out something like "it takes a sexually aroused man to make a chick affectionate.")

No longer do African-American women have to make do with "suntan" shades of foundation cosmetics intended for Caucasian skin. First small and then large companies have developed cosmetics that enhance the vast range of black skin tones and that don't make black women look ashen.

Flori Roberts, an entrepreneur, was a pioneer in cosmetics for African-Americans; big companies have also jumped on the money wagon. In 1991 Prescriptives, Estee Lauder's slickly packaged cosmetic brand aimed at urban working women, launched All Skins—makeup formulated for all skin colors—in a direct appeal to ethnic women and attracted almost four thousand new customers a month.

Although the often self-sufficient Chinatowns and Korea-towns still serve their communities, marketers are targeting these and other groups with goods and services designed and promoted with Asians' unique requirements and preferences in mind.

These previously untargeted minority markets spend billions of dollars annually. The total annual spending power of African- and Asian-American and Hispanic consumers is estimated at more than $500 billion dollars!

New Opportunities in Untapped Segments

Just as U.S. business learned in the 1970s and 1980s that a deep understanding of different cultures is necessary to sell overseas, in the 1990s companies are having to develop the same kind of multicultural awareness to compete successfully in the U.S. domestic market.

The mainstream market is wildly overtapped. While many companies have fought over slices of the tiny yuppie market, the mature market, the senior market, the women's market, and other slow-growth markets, they have ignored the ethnic market, the fastest-growing and the most profitable market of all.

Some say that these markets are made up primarily of poor people who are not worth targeting; others respond that this attitude smacks of conscious or unconscious racism. But those marketers who have targeted and captured a slice of the very sweet ethnic pie have profited enormously.

Look at Binney & Smith, the company that has enchanted generations of kids with Crayola crayons. Their "flesh" color had traditionally been a sort of beigy-pink. Many Americans, however, have darker shades of flesh. Although the company had other "fleshlike" tones of crayons, ranging from apricot to mahogany, in their sixty-four-pack, those colors weren't called "flesh." In the early 1990s, Binney & Smith came out with a pack of skin-tone crayons in their own box.

I have always wondered why manufacturers of bandages spent so many years selling pink bandages to Americans of all colors before discovering that clear bandages look good on all skin tones. Late in 1992 one small company also came out with brown-toned bandages.

A brand of panty hose called Afrotique is sold in Pueblo supermarkets in the U.S. Virgin Islands, where the population is predominantly African-American. The panty hose are sold in all the traditional shades of beige, brown, and black. The stores also sell the beigy-pink called nude by many mainstream marketers of panty hose, but Afrotique simply calls it light beige.

Major companies such as Procter & Gamble, Anheuser-Busch, and Campbell's spent $734 million in 1991 for ad campaigns that targeted only Hispanics. And companies such as J. C. Penney, Mattel, Pillsbury, and Quaker Oats spent more than $750 million advertising to African-Americans in 1992.

Mainstream companies such as Revlon, Maybelline, and Estee Lauder, with their cosmetics for black, Hispanic, and Asian women, see the strong advantages of marketing to ethnic and minority customers. Although sales of standard cosmetic products in the $4 billion cosmetics industry are barely growing at 3 percent a year, some new smaller lines aimed at minorities have increased sales by as much as 25 percent annually.

Developing cosmetics for ethnic and minority women is an especially good idea when we realize that the median age for Caucasians is almost thirty-three, while the median age for black and Hispanics is far younger. And younger customers are more likely to try new products, according to Lafayette Jones, president of Segmented Marketing Services, Inc., a marketing company in Winston-Salem, North Carolina.

U.S. companies that learn about the tastes and preferences of the ethnic markets within this country are also finding an extra benefit; they can use their new knowledge to enter overseas markets in the Pacific Rim and in Latin America, where there is great pent-up consumer demand for U.S. goods.

For some companies, it works the other way. Greg Walker, marketing communications manager at Eastman Kodak in Rochester, New York, says, "Like many companies, we had a global focus before we had an ethnic focus. That experience provided valuable insights for reaching different segments of the domestic market."

The Impact of Immigration

Even if a company doesn't export, its domestic market is increasingly made up of foreign-born consumers. The U.S. population will continue to be reshaped by millions of immigrants and their children through the rest of the 1990s and into the twenty-first century. Many workers will be immigrants, and many immigrants will open their own businesses. The strongest impact of immigration will continue to be on the East and West Coasts, but the changes will be felt nationwide.

Clearly, immigration is reconfiguring the U.S. population. Not only are immigrants (legal and illegal) coming here in record numbers, they are also coming from a more diverse group of countries. Chinese immigrants have been joined by Cambodians, Laotians, Vietnamese, Indonesians, Pakistanis, and Thais; Mexicans, by Guatemalans, Peruvians, Salvadorans, and Ecuadorans.

Increased immigration and higher fertility rates among blacks, Hispanics, and Asians led the Census Bureau in 1992 to revise a 1989 population forecast that there would be fewer than 300 million people in the United States by 2050; the new projection raised that estimate to 383 million.

Although the percentage of children in the United States as a whole is declining, blacks, Hispanics, and Asians are having more children per family than are their white counterparts. Blacks represent 15 percent of children under five years old, and Hispanics represent 12 percent. By 2010 more than 33 percent of American children will be minorities.

Immigration in the 1990s will be greater than in the 1980s. A total of eight to ten million legal and illegal immigrants will have arrived by the end of the decade, and by 2010 there will be nearly 35 million foreign-born people in the United States.

Benefits of Immigration

Savvy marketers want to sell to immigrants, simply because there are so many, regardless of their personal feeling about immigration policy. But nativists, such as the 1992 presidential candidate Pat Buchanan, who want "America for Americans" (and only some Americans, at that), are basing their arguments on stereotypes, not on hard facts.

Although impoverished immigrants do put a strain on the social welfare system, few Americans notice that the number of skilled, working, tax-paying immigrants has been increasing along with the number of needy immigrants. About one quarter of immigrant workers are college graduates, slightly higher than the proportion among native-born Americans. The 11 million working immigrants earn at least $240 billion a year and pay almost $100 billion in taxes, more than covering the estimated $5 billion that legal immigrants receive in welfare payments.

Most immigrants do not take jobs away from native-born Americans; often they create jobs. Immigrant entrepreneurs are opening businesses of all sizes. Businesses run by immigrants from Asia, for example, have ready-made connections overseas and have made big contributions to the U.S. export boom. But immigrant small-business owners create jobs, too, and not only for other immigrants.

The next generation of scientists and engineers at U.S. high-tech companies will be dominated by immigrants. While the number of native-born Americans getting science Ph.D.s has not changed since 1980, the number of foreign-born students receiving doctorates in science more than doubled between 1981 and 1991, when they accounted for 37 percent of the total. And about 51 percent of computer science doctorates in 1991 went to foreign-born students.

An economic benefit that is not often heard about is the contribution the new immigrants make to American cities. Immigrants are usually drawn to major metropolitan areas, where they often breathe new life into cities and older suburbs by opening businesses, paying taxes, and buying goods and services.

Some nearly abandoned neighborhoods in the inner cities have been brought back to life by immigrants looking for cheap housing. In the 1980s the populations of America's ten largest cities grew by 4.7 percent; without immigrants they would have shrunk by 6.8 percent, according to *Business Week* magazine.

Managing Diversity

Changes in the workforce brought about by immigration have already been felt. According to the U.S. Department of Labor, native white men account for only 45 percent of America's almost 120 million workers. By the late 1990s that share will decline to 39 percent. Although the labor force will grow slowly as we approach the year 2000, two thirds of the increase will be made up of women starting or returning to work; minority males and immigrants will account for much of the rest. Only 9.3 percent of the new workers will represent the population from which nearly all top corporate managers have sprung: white, non-Hispanic, U.S.-born men. An entire industry on managing diversity, which offers seminars, workshops, guidebooks, and videos to corporate human resources departments, has emerged to sensitize management to the rapid changes in America's working population.

From Melting Pot to Mosaic

Not only are minority groups increasing in size, they are also not assimilating the way many minority and ethnic (especially immigrant) groups did in the past. The largely European immigrants in the early 1900s pushed their children to blend in, assimilate, and be "American"; schools insisted that only English be spoken, and children could be punished by both teachers and parents for speaking their native language. Not only did many children forget most of their cultural heritage, they were often happy to do so.

In contrast, some of the new immigrants find it more difficult to blend in than did earlier groups that were primarily white and European. And there is far less pressure on them to do so.

Our cultural model is becoming the mosaic, not the melting pot. Since the civil rights struggles of the 1960s, many groups are choosing ethnic pride, separatism, and even militance. Some recent arrivals aren't willing to join the mainstream but prefer the old language and ways. If you are considering selling to them, you must be aware of these issues and design your marketing mix to reflect it.

The issue of assimilation is a very complex one and affects different ethnic groups differently. "You won't find Hispanics at Taco Bell," according to George Rosenbaum, CEO of Leo J. Shapiro & Associates, a market research company in Chicago. "You'll find Hispanics and other second-generation ethnics eating cheeseburgers at McDonald's."

Some African-Americans have chosen not to push the assimilation and integration process and prefer to associate mostly with other African-Americans. Radamase Cabrera, an urban planner for Washington, D.C., chooses to live in the nearby affluent black suburb of Prince George's County, Maryland. Quoted in *The New York Times Magazine*, Cabrera says, "Why should I beg some cracker to integrate me into his society when he doesn't want to? Why keep beating my head up against a wall?"

Similarly, there are communities in New York, San Francisco, and other cities where Chinese-Americans go to school, marry, and live almost their entire lives without speaking to a non-Chinese. On the other hand, there are large numbers of Chinese-Americans who integrate into mainstream communities and assimilate almost completely in accordance with the standard rule of thumb that assimilation takes place by the third generation.

Assimilation is not an either/or. It's a continuum, and marketers must deal with varying degrees of assimilation within any ethnic market. Companies need to be aware of each subgroup's pattern of assimilation and then determine whether it's cost-effective to target these segments with specific marketing campaigns.

Targeting Minority Segments

There are many ways to target immigrant markets. Chemical Bank has installed Russian-language automated teller machines at its branch in Brighton Beach, Brooklyn, to capture the business of the large numbers of Russians who have moved to Brighton Beach, only half-jokingly referred to as Little Odessa by the Sea.

In California, Vons supermarkets decided to develop a separate chain to cater specifically to Hispanic customers, especially first-generation immigrants. The nine Tianguis (an Aztec word for marketplace) stores in southern California sell cuts of meat popular in Mexico—such as fresh beef lips and pig snouts—and products imported from Mexico.

Another example is New York Downtown Hospital, near Manhattan's Chinatown. It appeals to Chinese patients with picky palates by serving dishes like congee, or rice gruel, and bean curd with black bean sauce.

J. C. Penney, the retailer, test-marketed imported African women's clothing in twenty-two of its stores and now features African Collection in its catalogs.

However, sometimes all that may be needed to capture a new ethnic segment of the market is a change in the manner of advertising, promoting, or selling or a focus on customer service. Even more important, all that may be needed to capture a new market is to make a segment aware that the product exists.

To capture a market segment that doesn't read English well or that may not be aware of the range of financial services available in this country, Dreyfus Corporation, at its San Francisco investment center, offers a money market fund prospectus in Chinese. And the Colonial and Pioneer fund groups offer some sales literature in Spanish.

Blacks, Asians, and Hispanics are not the only segments that are out there spending money. The large gay and lesbian population, the disabled, and the growing number of traditionally observant Jews and Moslems are some of the powerful groups who no longer want to beg for products and services tailored and targeted to them.

Minorities' Growing Affluence

Not only are African-Americans, Asians, and Hispanics becoming more numerous in the U.S., they are also becoming more affluent, better educated, and more visible. Asian-Americans have the highest household incomes in the entire U.S. population, with a 1990 median income of $38,500. Hispanic income ranges from $31,500 for Cubans to $23,350 for Mexicans and $18,000 for Puerto Ricans. African-Americans earn a median income of $18,700 a year.

The proportion of college-age minorities attending colleges and universities increased between 1985 and 1990. Of African-American high school graduates, 33 percent were attending college in 1990, compared with 26.1 percent five years earlier, with most of the gains coming from women. The percentage of college-age Hispanics in attendance increased to 29 percent from 26.1 percent. (White attendance increased to 39.4 percent in 1990 from 34.4 percent in 1985.)

Ethnic Media

Ethnic media, and ethnics *in* the media, have reshaped our popular culture. In part because of the rise of advertising agencies owned or run by African-Americans, for example, we are seeing blacks in mainstream ads that were previously all-white.

Many major cities have at least one Spanish-language television station. The Black Entertainment Television (BET) channel is available to many cable subscribers, and in many large cities at least one channel shows Chinese and Korean programs. Magazines for every segment of the ethnic market abound, from *Ebony* and *Essence* and *Black Enterprise* to *Hispanic* and *Hispanic Business* to the Asian-American magazines *A*, *Transpacific*, and *Face* (for Asian-American women).

The Rising Influence of Boomers

Just as immigration and minority birthrates are bringing greater ethnic diversity to the American population, other demographic, cultural, and economic factors, such as the aging (and rising influence) of the baby-boom generation, are changing America in profound ways.

Somewhere around 75 million boomers, white, black, and brown and born between 1946 and 1964, will shape the country's buying behavior, as well as its social and political direction, at least until 2039, when the youngest boomers will turn seventy-five. There are no better examples of this than Bill Clinton and Al Gore, elected president and vice president, in 1992. True to his promise to make diversity part of his administration, President Clinton appointed "a cabinet that looks like America."

Steeped in the rhetoric of the civil rights movement of the 1960s and the feminist movement of the 1970s, boomers have embraced issues of diversity as has no other generation. This trend toward diversity has expanded the consciousness—and the palate—of the previously largely homogeneous Anglo-America. The fact that salsa now outsells ketchup is a result not only of the growing Hispanic market and its influence but of boomers' more adventuresome taste buds.

Changing Families

The rise of the baby-boom generation has been accompanied by great changes in the structure of American families. "Family" used to mean a white father who worked, a housewife, 2.3 kids, and a beagle. The increase in working women, the graying of America, the proliferation of single-parent households, and the increase in the minority population have all given us countless new profiles.

Today a family may mean an over-forty-five, single, minority working mother and her child or any other combination or permutation of people. Single parents head nearly 10 million households, and almost 55 million women are in the workforce, more than double the number in 1960. There are five times as many unmarried couples living together as there were in 1970. "Domestic partnerships" of unmarried couples, including same-sex couples, have been fighting for the same benefits and rights married couples always have had. In some states and municipalities, they are already receiving those benefits.

Households with children once defined the American mass market. Today, only about one U.S. household in three contains a child, and the number of nonfamily households is projected to grow even more rapidly in the mid-1990s.

But while households with children are now only one segment of a diverse population, for marketers they are very often the best segment; households with children spend more in almost every category of products and services. Increasingly, households with children are likely to be ethnic and minority households.

Regional Diversity

The demographic changes we have described are not happening uniformly in every regional market. New immigrants cluster in big cities and in areas where they have relatives and friends. Three out of every four new immigrants live in California, New York, Texas, Florida, Illinois, or New Jersey, with metro Los Angeles the top destination. Even in the suburbs, however, Asian and Hispanic populations grew sharply in the 1980s.

Different immigrant and minority groups cluster in different parts of the country. The political, social, and dollar power of the Cuban community in South Florida since the 1959 takeover of Cuba by Fidel Castro is the result of massive demographic changes in the region. Former Colorado Governor Richard Lamm observed, somewhat tongue in cheek, in *The Wall Street Journal* that "demographers are academics who can statistically prove that the average person in Miami is born Cuban and dies Jewish."

No other area in America has been so transformed by immigrants as Miami. A sleepy tourist area thirty-five years ago, Miami now has more foreign-born residents than any other major U.S. city. Hispanics constitute 49 percent of Dade County's 1.9 million residents. Latinization has transformed not only Miami but most of South Florida and even parts of Georgia and Virginia. Florida's total minority population, which includes not only Hispanics but substantial numbers of African-Americans, Haitians, and others, is close to 30 percent.

In the South, African-Americans have gained far greater political, economic, and social power than they have elsewhere in the United States, with Atlanta being the heart of this power bloc. Many of the politicians, religious and educational leaders, and businesspeople who have redefined the South are African-Americans. But the clout of the African-American community is by no means limited to the South.

In the West and the Southwest, the influence of Mexican-Americans is increasingly being felt. From a historical perspective, there is a certain irony in this, because much of the Southwest was once owned by Mexico. Today, Mexicans are, in effect, reclaiming parts of the territory they believe was unfairly seized by the United States. In New Mexico, where the first European settlers were sixteenth-century Spaniards, whites without Hispanic backgrounds account for barely half the population.

Mexicans, Guatemalans, Salvadorans, and other Hispanics in the early 1990s made up more than 37 percent of the population of Los Angeles County and more than 25 percent of the population of the state of California. A total of 44 percent of the population of Los Angeles was foreign-born, although not all of these immigrants were Hispanic. According to the 1990 census, the state of California was 57 percent Caucasian (keep in mind that this figure includes most Hispanics).

In New York City, Hispanics in 1990 were the largest minority group, surpassing blacks. Minority residents of all backgrounds made up more than 31 percent of New York state's population. In New Jersey, the total minority population rose to 26 percent and in Connecticut, 16 percent, according to the 1990 census. There were more Asian-Americans in New York (694,000) than in Hawaii (685,000).

The rise of Asian influence in the West and the Pacific Northwest can be felt in many ways. The cover of *Transpacific* magazine, published in Los Angeles, trumpeted that "by the year 2000, 75 percent of Californians will be working for an Asian-owned business or paying rent to an Asian landlord." Although that projection is open to question, it is at the very least a sign of the Asian community's perception of its growing importance in the region.

The most successful businesses in the coming years will be the ones that make the effort to understand that ethnic and other segmentation—appealing to the tastes and preferences of different groups—is the key to profitability. Those marketers with the vision to develop product and market strategies to appeal to the coming "new majority" will be the ones that prosper.

2

Segmenting a Diverse Market

For years the debate has raged: Is marketing an art or a science? I vote for art. True, there are quantifiable aspects of the marketing process—especially the research—and we certainly need to design and interpret data accurately, but, for me, the heart of marketing lies with those creative, arty types who have vision.

Building a better mousetrap will get **your** mice trapped more efficiently, but how can potential customers benefit from your genius if they don't know the item you're promoting exists? Contrary to the old saying, the world will not beat a path to your door unless it *knows* that you've built a better mousetrap and, more important, knows what's better about it. That's where the art comes in.

Of course, you could spend years learning this art. This chapter is not a definitive guide to marketing but an overview of some general marketing techniques and research methods.

The Heart of Marketing

Definitions of marketing range from "the satisfaction of needs and wants at a reasonable price" to "a total system of interacting business activities to plan, price, promote, and distribute want-satisfying products and services to household and organizational users at a profit"; there are other definitions equally mind-numbing. They all come down to the same thing: Stimulate interest, create desire, and get the consumer to buy.

The heart of marketing has always been "know thy product and know thy market." Not only are we seeing rapid developments in the types of products and services that are available (how many ads for fax machines, video games, and overnight mail delivery services can you remember from your childhood?), but the markets themselves are so different from those of twenty years ago that many of the tried and true techniques of marketing are no longer valid.

The Marketing Mix

Marketing consists of four components, sometimes called the Four Ps: Product, Price, Place (distribution), and Promotion. Although you can often use a single overall marketing strategy, even in a diverse society like ours, you will almost always have to adjust one or more of these four Ps to reach ethnic and minority segments. Most often, that component will be promotion—for example, whether to advertise in foreign-language or minority media. But don't ignore the issues of product adaptation, pricing, and place (where and how goods are distributed).

Market Research and the Information Industry

Over the years, marketing research and strategy techniques have proliferated, so much so that there has been some backlash at the high price—in dollars, time, and personnel required—to perform what used to be basic data-gathering tasks. The explosion in technology has added a new dimension to what used to be rather straightforward techniques for determining what the customer wants and how to best reach him or her; today, you can buy all manner of computerized databases and cross-tabulate the cross-tabulations! We have so many ways to dissect the consuming public that it's easy to get confused after a while. In fact, we have overreached the general market at the expense of the ethnic and minority segments.

Having access to information isn't bad; in fact, it can help us as marketers better determine who the customer is, where he or she lives, and how to position the product properly. But having access to the information is useless if we don't use it properly. Never has the slogan "garbage in, garbage out" been more applicable than in marketing.

It's not enough to know how to use information technology properly; we must learn to ask relevant questions, track trends, evaluate data, and anticipate change—in short, keep our eyes and ears open. Clearly, the customer mix is changing. To prosper, we must be able to reach our market segments with the right mix of culturally appropriate products, pricing, promotion, positioning, and distribution channels.

Because the practice of marketing and the marketing mix are continually reinventing themselves, there are plenty of ways to get the world to beat a path to the door of our NEW! IMPROVED! MOUSETRAP!

We already know that the *product,* the first component, is the newest and the best, but what about the price, the place or distribution channel, and the promotion and positioning? What components of our marketing mix do we need to adjust to appeal to diverse segments of the market? We need to learn who the customer is and what the customer wants from the products. We need to focus on the benefit sought by the customer, not on the features of the product.

What Does the Customer Want?

People buy what the product or service can *do* for them, not what the product and its features *are.* Different people want different things from the same product. So before we try to sell, let's first find out what the customers want and what they want our products and services to do for them.

In the mousetrap case, it's easy. Most people don't care how the mouse is caught, only that it is caught. With the exception of one segment of our diverse culture, the animal rights activists, most consumers view mice as unwanted in the home and associate them with dirt and disease.

To sell to animal rights activists, it's vital to stress humane treatment of the mouse. In fact, one savvy manufacturer, Pied Piper International of Salem, New Hampshire, has come out with the $1.99 Mice Cube, which traps the animal harmlessly so that it can be set free. But for most people, reliability and the guarantee that the mouse will be caught or killed are the primary benefits.

Who buys mousetraps—poor people, rural people, city dwellers, rich people, suburbanites, immigrants? All of the above. But would you advertise your great invention in the same place to reach all of them? Since your market for mousetraps includes everyone from rich people with vacation homes in the country to immigrants living in squalid tenements, you must aim separately at every segment.

If you advertise your mousetrap only in mainstream media and ignore minority or foreign-language broadcast and print media, if you sell it only in hardware and specialty stores and not in supermarkets or ethnic neighborhood shops, if the package and directions are in technical jargon and not in plain English or pictures, you may be missing a large percentage of your potential market.

Sometimes, advertising isn't the answer to reaching a segment. A program of community education at a local organization or association will make minority consumers aware of your product. An educational program in which influential community leaders or small-business owners are given the mousetrap free to use in their own homes and businesses is a great way to introduce your product.

Positive word of mouth is always a marketer's dream, but in many ethnic and minority communities, it's especially valuable. Just one recommendation from an important person in the community may be enough to clear the shelves of mousetraps.

Customer-Driven Marketing

Although many products are perceived and used in the same way by different consumers, sometimes the same product can provide different benefits for different people. Our goal as marketers is to match our products and services to our customer's needs. This approach is known as customer-driven marketing.

By learning what the consumer wants and by customizing our products, services, and marketing communications efforts, we make greater profits through customer satisfaction than we would with the "here's what we make, how can we offload it" approach.

Segments and Niches

Some marketers go so far as to say that we should strive to individualize marketing to the point that we sell to a market of one. Whether it will ever be cost-effective to "micromarket," to aim for a segment of one, is not yet clear.

That uncertainty is no reason not to target customers as precisely as possible, aiming not for the whole market but for slices of the pie, or segments, and for the even narrower groups, slices of slices, called niches. When we target our marketing in this way, we see that some of these segments have, until recently, been overwhelmingly ignored, especially ethnic and minority consumers.

Primary and Secondary Market Research

Clearly, we need to do a good deal of research, whether we represent a large company or a small one, a company that is well-established or a new venture. Here's where we gather our information on individuals and organizations; record, analyze, and interpret it; and then apply the findings to target the customer. We can use primary research, which involves interviews, questionnaires, focus groups, and sampling, or secondary research, where we gather information from directories, guides, periodicals, and sometimes even our competitors.

But how do we understand what the customer really wants and needs? Will our questionnaires and surveys give us the

information to provide the right products, services, and promotional mix for our market? Are our research methods culturally relevant to the segment we're targeting?

In fact, are we doing the research at all? Assuming we are
aware of our corporate objectives and capabilities, we need to
get research on our target market that is relevant and designed
specifically for this new market.

For example, standard research questionnaires, even when
translated accurately into Spanish or Chinese, may not work
because many immigrants are not comfortable with the very
American practice of giving out nearly any information asked
for. Telephone interviews may not be useful with Hispanics
unless interviewers are Hispanic themselves or are completely
fluent in Spanish. The whole concept of using "standard techniques" is flawed, since most of the the models are based on
Anglo-American consumer values. Although some Hispanics
and Asians will give out information on the telephone, depend-
ing on their degree of assimilation, they often prefer a face-to-
face interview. If the person being questioned is a recent
immigrant, he or she may fear that the interviewers are from
"the government" or that any information given may be used
against the interviewee in some way.

Observational Research

It's a good idea either to have market researchers who are
highly knowledgeable about the market or to hire an ethnic or
minority research firm. The standard research techniques used
for the mainstream market may not be useful with African-
American, Asian, or Hispanic customers because of the tremendous differences in lifestyle, values, and frames of reference. Research needs to be adapted to the lifestyle and the
values of the segment in question, or else the data gathered
will be virtually worthless.

One useful technique that is relatively inexpensive and
that works well with many segments is observational research,
getting out into the field and watching what is going on.
Observational research often uncovers much more information

than traditional research techniques and may prove to be more accurate, especially when studying ethnic and minority customers.

Some companies have hired anthropologists, ethnologists, and sociologists to go out and watch how people do things. Most people, including mainstream customers, don't report accurately when they fill out questionnaires. They usually offer either idealized answers or what they think is the right answer.

A number of years ago, one consumer goods company had a television ad showing a woman washing dishes by dunking them in a sinkful of soapy water and then rinsing them off by dunking them in a sinkful of clear water. The campaign was less than successful. Observational research showed that, except during a drought, most people wash dishes under running water. Now that environmental conservation has become a driving national issue, we may soon see such ads again. But for the meantime, ads should reflect the reality of how products are used, because we know that people are more likely to buy products if they can identify with the individual using them or the situation.

Demographics, Geographics, and Psychographics

Along with observing what people do and how they do it, we need to look at demographics (age, income, gender), geographics (region, state, city and neighborhood), and psychographics (personality characteristics).

Values and Lifestyles (or VALS) was a popular technique, used in the early 1980s, for describing people in terms of broad categories, such as "achievers," "emulators," or "belongers." VALS has fallen out of favor because companies found it wasn't detailed enough, and today few marketers use psychographics without combining it with other segmentation techniques.

In the early 1980s, Joel Garreau's *The Nine Nations of North America* gave us a new way of looking at regional marketing. His technique segmented the United States, Canada, and Mexico into nine separate regions; the distinguishing features of each region were shown, and a capital city was designated to head up each one. For example, "MexAmerica," with Los Angeles as its capital, included southwestern and central California, southern Arizona, western New Mexico, southern Texas, and southern Colorado and Mexico, where, because these regions share an ethnic heritage, Mexican tastes, culture, and influence are strongly felt.

Marketers have long known that tastes, usage, and purchasing patterns differ regionally. But some companies found that using regional market strategies was both complex and costly. New techniques, however, allow for more precise targeting of regional marketing.

Martha Farnsworth Riche reported on the marriage of demographics and geographics in *American Demographics* magazine: "Geodemographic systems place each neighborhood, based on zip code plus four-digits or 'cluster' that includes its statistically similar peers. Each cluster is labeled and rated according to its affluence or market potential."

Tony Adams, director of market planning at Campbell's Soup, explained in a 1987 interview that Campbell's had tried putting much more of a jalapeño pepper "hit" to their nacho cheese soup in the Southwest than in the rest of the country. But Campbell's soon learned of fast-growing pockets of jalapeño pepper lovers in the Northeast and other parts of the country, and adjusted the recipe.

Using information derived from each decade's census, the Claritas Corporation has dreamed up hilarious categories for labeling zip-code neighborhoods. Pools and Patios, Sun-Belt Singles, Shotguns and Pickups, and Ethnic Row Houses are typical categories. Joining zip code 10021, which covers New York's affluent silk stocking district, including Park and Fifth avenues, in the top-drawer category is Beverly Hills 90210. Claritas would call these neighborhoods Urban Gold Coasts.

Now, we are seeing further segmentation of this system into census block groups of as few as 350 households. This twist on "you are where you live" give marketers a great deal of information about potential customers' wants and needs. Some marketers feel sure that, controversy aside, they can target the buyers for malt liquor just as well as they can for imported champagnes.

Computer geographic information systems (GIS) have spawned a whole new industry. GIS uses census and other important demographic, economic, and sales data to create digitized, color maps that can illustrate market conditions and identify areas of opportunity and saturation. GIS software can create color maps that spotlight neighborhoods where ethnics and minorities are concentrated. Other variables, such as household size and loctions of competitors, can be added.

In another twist, Standard Rate and Data Service, in Oak Brook, Illinois, has developed a database that combines zip code information with lifestyle information.

Segmentation that works must be quantifiable (e.g., by market size, sales, share of market, profits, potential customers), must create markets large enough to represent a profitable business activity, and must identify customer pools in which the product or service can maintain a sustainable competitive advantage.

Self-Identification and Segmentation

Many African-Americans feel that the lifestyle situations and the traditional blonde, blue-eyed wholesomeness of the models in many ads are so irrelevant to them that they tune out the message completely. It's not surprising that they are completely uninterested in the product being pitched.

Companies that succeed know that, within the ethnic and minority communities, there are different segments that need to be reached in very different ways. These companies segment their target market into a set of potential buyers who have common needs and who are alike in the way they perceive the product, value it, buy it, and use it.

Segmentation analysis is especially effective for products that focus on the consumer's lifestyle and self-image. A few years ago, Coca-Cola segmented its ads to Hispanics by including the "comfort" food appropriate to the Mexican, Cuban, and Puerto Rican segments in its ads.

Coors beer tailors locations, music, and casting of models in regions that have a dominant Hispanic segment. Playing

Mexican ranchera music instead of Puerto Rican salsa during a segment aimed at Puerto Ricans would send the message that Coors saw all Hispanics as being the same. Or the company might be perceived as not caring enough about its Puerto Rican customers to play the right music for them.

Many upscale African-Americans justifiably resent being targeted with ads that they feel are more suitable to downscale customers. And if potential customers don't have positive feelings toward a company, obviously they won't buy its products. Such resentment can result in bottom-line losses for a company, especially because negative word of mouth travels even faster than positive word of mouth.

This kind of stereotyping is not limited to the African-American or Hispanic consumer. Dr. Diane Simpson, president of Simpson International in New York City, a marketing firm specializing in the Asian market, says, "When promoting products and services to Asians, avoid using phony orientally shaped English letters in the text, which is especially irritating to Japanese- and Korean-Americans." Along with being patronizing and lumping the many diverse groups of Asians together, the use of such a typeface projects the idea that, to the company, all Asians identify with their Asian-ness to the same degree.

In the same way that marketers have moved from mass marketing to segmented marketing in mainstream America, they must segment ethnic and minority markets, as well.

Targeting and Positioning

After determining which market segments to target, we need to position our products and services. Tropical Fantasy is a big seller to immigrants from the Caribbean, who favor its low-priced, fruit-flavored sodas. Eric Miller is the owner of the Brooklyn Bottling Company, which markets Best Health natural fruit sodas and juices to an upscale segment of the market. He is also the licensee for a top Jamaican soda company and is targeting West Indian immigrants who say the inexpensive soda's fruity taste reminds them of home. If the total market is soda drinkers and one segment of that market is minority soda drinkers, Miller is targeting a niche of primarily West Indian immigrants. He positions the soda as providing the taste of the tropics (home, to his customers) and uses its low price to differentiate it from the competition. Miller is going after a different niche or subsegment of the ethnic market with an apple-flavored drink, which is a favorite of Colombians and is popular among other Latin American immigrants. Clearly, companies of all sizes can profit from innovating, adapting, positioning, retrofitting, and promoting goods and services for ethnic and minority consumers.

The Product Life Cycle

Today, given the deluge of credit cards, it seems hard to imagine that in the 1970s some credit card issuers discouraged single women from applying for credit cards. That was before they realized what a lucrative market they were missing. With the same kind of thinking, some companies today are still avoiding or ignoring the ethnic or minority market.

Especially in a sluggish economy, companies need to find ways to extend the life cycles of their products or services in markets that are oversaturated or when the product is in maturity. To do this, new users and new uses need to be found for the product. Sometimes stimulating more usage by existing consumers is the answer. But targeting a previously ignored segment of the ethnic market usually provides the greatest return on investment.

Bank of America was able to attract new depositors by targeting Mexican and Central American immigrants. These customers were not responding to mainstream advertising because most of them had no experience with banks and didn't understand what an interest-bearing account was, according to Ennio Quevado-Garcia, the bank's vice president and manager of market segments. The bank now spends a lot of time and money educating different immigrant groups about banking services and making bank branches less intimidating to immigrant customers.

Another successful example of a campaign to expand a product's life cycle is Goya Food's effort to expand the market for foods it has sold for years to the Puerto Rican and other Hispanic markets. Goya, one of the East Coast's largest producers and distributors of canned and packaged beans and other specialties, has recently crossed over and introduced its beans and other products to mainstream non-Hispanic America. To capitalize on the diverse palates of the baby boomers and others, Goya's new ads include delicious recipes that grab attention in publications like *The New York Times*, with the banner CHICK PEAS: BEYOND THE SALAD BAR.

Without endangering its fiercely loyal following in the Hispanic market, Goya is positioning itself to capture a whole new mainstream market. It's not disloyal to sell to one segment of the market while attempting to capture another; it's just good business sense. It simply requires vastly different advertising and promotional strategies.

Building Brand Loyalty

Some observers have claimed that ethnic and minority consumers, particularly Hispanics, are more loyal to national leading brands than are other consumers, perhaps because Hispanics lack awareness of "follower" or second-tier brands. Many competitive brands don't have the funds to advertise to ethnically segmented markets or may not think it's cost-efficient. In contrast to the general market, which is exposed by media advertising to the entire spectrum of competing products, many Hispanics, Asian-, and African-Americans are not aware of possibilities other than the leading national brand.

It's worth gold to show that your company has products or services specifically targeted to the segment you're trying to capture. Consumers who have positive feelings about the company that makes a product are likely to buy the product. So go the extra mile and develop, package, position, and promote goods to the intended audience.

Cause Marketing

A great way to appeal to ethnic and minority customers is through "cause marketing" that benefits a cause that is favored by the group you wish to reach. For example, a national or regional advertising campaign can offer to contribute one dollar to a charity such as the United Negro College fund or ASPIRA (a scholarship fund for Hispanics) every time someone makes a purchase. On a local level, companies can sponsor a parade or a religious festival, make a donation to a playground or a youth league, or help other worthy causes.

One excellent way to appeal to both ethnics and upscale consumers is to support the organizations that fight for environmental justice. The *People of Color Environmental Groups Directory* lists 205 minority organizations with an environmental focus. These are groups of ethnics and minorities that are united against pollution and dumping, which seem to occur frequently in poor neighborhoods where land is cheap and political clout is low. This is the kind of sponsorship that gets written about in magazines as diverse as *Ebony* and *Natural History*.

These are only some of the ways successful companies can create awareness for their products and services. You'll be surprised how much goodwill you can generate—especially in a tightly knit ethnic neighborhood—even with a limited promotional outlay.

3

The Importance of Culture in Marketing

With all of the brainwork that goes into developing a strategic marketing plan, you might think that the last thing marketers need to deal with is cross-cultural and ethnicity issues. Wrong! It's the *first* thing that we need to look at if we want to prosper in the late 1990s and into the next century. Marketers who spend their time and resources learning about the cultural differences (and similarities) among consumers and who use that knowledge to develop products, promotions, and distribution strategies will become industry leaders.

Culture

What is this thing called culture that we keep hearing about? Culture is what gives us our identity and the code of conduct that we live by. It is learned, shared, and passed on from one generation to the next, by families, by religious institutions, by schools and governments. Culture is learned behavior that distinguishes members of a society and includes what the group thinks, says, and does.

Mainstream U.S. culture stresses the importance of the individual, prizes informal, direct, and open communication, believes that "time is money," sharply delineates the time for work and for play, highly values the concept of self-help, desires change, seeks to get ahead of the competition, believes in the egalitarian ideal, and emphasizes material gain.

Other cultures may be rooted in totally opposite beliefs and behaviors. Our job as marketers is to understand the differences, not to judge them.

Understanding Minority Segments

How do we begin to unravel the differences so that we can design successful marketing programs for ethnic and minority markets that will give a satisfactory return on investment? According to Larry Glover, executive vice president of J. Curtis & Co. in Montclair, New Jersey, "If you reach the African-American market with the right mix of product and promotion, the bottom line is a much higher return on investment than you would achieve in the general market. But the key issue here is that of making critical decisions about ethnic marketing without knowledge of ethnics. Companies would not do that in any other phase of business."

Although no one expects every marketer to be an anthropologist, sociologist, or ethnologist, we need to learn how cultural issues of language, religion, family patterns, gender roles, education, and aspirations affect consumer behavior patterns. Whether we obtain this information from books, by taking courses, or by bringing in experts (or by any combination of these) is not the issue. What's important is that the information is obtained with sensitivity through a structured format by qualified managers.

What's needed is the same kind of research that is done for the general market. Only then can we analyze whether to change or adapt the product or service, the promotional mix, or the channels of distribution. But we must take cultural differences into consideration when designing all aspects of the marketing mix.

High- and Low-Context Cultures

Dr. Edward Hall, an anthropologist who has spent many years writing and teaching about intercultural behavioral differences and their applications to business, spoke about how some of his colleagues working on a road project during the Depression of the 1930s had trouble communicating with Native Americans, even though they all spoke English. His colleagues, Dr. Hall explained, held a "deficit model" of the unfamiliar behavior they encountered—that is, they saw Native American patterns of behavior as defective or inferior, rather than as simply different.

Dr. Hall, who has spent many years as consultant to major corporations and who wrote about cultural issues in business for the *Harvard Business Review* as early as 1960, divides cultures into high-context and low-context cultures. Communication in a high-context culture depends heavily on the context, or nonverbal aspects of communication; low-context cultures depend more on explicit, verbally expressed communication. According to Hall, the United States is a low-context culture, relying heavily on information communicated explicitly by words. Asian and Hispanic cultures, by contrast, are high-context cultures.

Janet Davis, a Princeton, New Jersey, consultant specializing in minority issues, says, "African-American culture is highly stratified and regionalized. Southern blacks are very traditional and tend to be higher-context than northern blacks. There are also tremendous class differences regionally and generationally."

African-Americans sometimes span two cultures. A black lawyer friend of mine says that during the week he works in the mainstream Anglo-American world wearing pin stripes and speaking highly educated legalese. On weekends he occasionally listens to rap music and speaks "blackspeak" with his friends.

Nonverbal Communication

In low-context cultures such as the United States and Germany, communication is mostly verbal and written. Very little information about the culture is communicated nonverbally. In high-context cultures, in contrast, a good deal of the communicating process occurs nonverbally. Body language, status, tonality, relationships and family, the use of silence, and many other factors communicate meaning.

But that doesn't mean that American culture doesn't allow for nonverbal communication. Mainstream Americans interpret gestures, silences, eye contact, and facial expressions in ways learned at home or at school. For example, most children in the United States are taught to look at the teacher or parent when they are being scolded. In many Asian, Latin American, Caribbean, and other cultures, in contrast, children are often taught to look down or away as a sign of respect for the person who is scolding them. Adult Americans regard someone who doesn't look them in the eye as shifty or untrustworthy, but most Asians think that looking someone in the eye is rude or confrontational. Similarly, people in mainstream America learn to smile broadly as a sign of friendliness or openness; in other cultures smiling may be considered false, overbearing, or worse.

A dramatic example of how gestures can be misinterpreted, with a devastating outcome, emerged during the 1992 riot in Los Angeles. Some of the African-Americans interviewed discussed their angry feelings toward Korean-American shop owners. They said they felt poorly treated because the Koreans didn't look them in the eye, smile at them, or put change from a purchase in their hand. The African-Americans interpreted the Korean-Americans' behavior as disrespectful.

Although Koreans are somewhat more outspoken than other Asians, they still consider it rude or aggressive to look deeply into someone's eyes, inappropriate or false to smile at someone they don't know very well, and improper to touch a stranger. If they are to succeed as retailers in the United States, however, they must learn that it's vital to take into account the cultural currency of the community. The Korean shopkeepers will have to adapt to the communication style of the culture of their customers in order to succeed for the long term. In Chicago, to help bridge intercultural gaps, the United Way has hired Karen Gunn, a highly trained black woman, to help African- and Korean-Americans understand one another. Gunn works in the community to teach Koreans to smile and to put change directly into a customer's hand, and she mediates minor disputes between the two groups.

My own experience while delivering marketing training to a group of Russian and Korean managers some years ago illustrates the explosive potential of misunderstandings between groups. A Russian manager had knocked over his overstuffed briefcase, which had been perched precariously on the edge of a desk. The Korean manager standing next to him began making a high-pitched, tittering sound that the Russian interpreted as laughing. The Russian turned beet-red and screamed, "You think is funny, is not funny." He pushed the Korean out of his way to begin picking up the pencils and paper that had fallen from the briefcase.

Fortunately, I knew that the Korean was not laughing at the Russian. The tittering with his hand over his mouth indicated that he was embarrassed or distressed at what had happened. I hoped that my negotiating skills would be sufficiently diplomatic, and I told the Russian that the Korean wasn't laughing at him but that he felt badly. The Korean instantly piped up, "Oh yes, badly, very badly."

I bent down and began picking up the pencils and papers, and before the Russian could say another word, the Korean speedily bent and picked up the rest of the papers and handed them to the Russian.

Another flashpoint for nonverbal communication or miscommunication is the concept of space. In some parts of the world the sense of personal space is totally different from the sense of space in the United States. As a result, some Latin Americans, for example, feel that Americans are cold, distant people simply because Americans' "comfort" distance is greater than theirs and Americans don't touch one another.

In one study, conversations in outdoor cafes in different countries were observed. The number of casual touches (of self or of the other party) per hour were counted. A total of 180 touches per hour were recorded in San Juan, Puerto Rico; two per hour were observed in Florida, and none at all in an hour in London.

Understanding these and other differences can be vital in determining the outcome of an ethnic marketing campaign.

Unless we are aware of these differences, the messages and intentions can be misunderstood.

Advertising and Context

In the United States, most advertising is low-context. It traditionally relies on words to explain the product and its features and how the product differs from the competition. By comparison, ads used in high-context countries such as Japan and Mexico rely on nuances and overall differences in the tone, music, style of dress of the actors, scenery, and other nonverbal cues to differentiate the product.

According to Dr. Diane Simpson of Simpson International in New York, "People from low-context cultures are often puzzled by high-context ads and wonder 'What's the point?' Whereas those from high-context cultures are more likely to say the ad taught them something worth remembering and made it easier for them to choose what brand to buy next time." She adds, "People from high-context cultures often find low-context ads pushy and aggressive, whereas those from low-context cultures often find them informative and persuasive."

One attempt to use a high-context ad in a low-context culture caused tremendous confusion in the United States when it was first introduced in 1989. Remember the Zen-like ads for the Infiniti by Nissan, which consisted of rocks and water and hills? Many consumers were frustrated by not seeing the car or hearing about its specifications and kept asking, "Where's the beef?" But when they finally saw the cars in later ads, their interest had already been aroused, and some people actively sought out the car.

Selling in a Foreign Language

One of the most basic cultural considerations is language. In the United States, there are millions of people who either speak no English at all or speak very little of it. If you're advertising in ethnic media, therefore, make sure the translation is correct for the subsegment you want to reach. And make sure your products and services are accessible to the target market.

United Airlines, which expanded its service to Latin America in 1992, operates a Spanish-speaking reservations line. The estimated number of calls on the line is about 450 a day. Imagine losing 450 consumers of your product because it was inaccessible to them! And, just to "let their fingers do the walking," there are Russian, Chinese, Iranian, Spanish, Korean, and other foreign-language yellow pages directories available.

Once you attract non-English speaking customers with your ad, however, you have to follow through. Customers who speak only Spanish or Chinese and who buy your product because of a newspaper ad in their native language will be frustrated and resentful if, when they get the product home, they find that the owner's manual is in English. In an extreme case, one manufacturer was sued by an injured consumer in Florida because the company heavily advertised the product in Spanish ads aimed at Hispanic buyers but put the label warning of the product's dangers only in English.

Time

One important cultural difference observed by Edward Hall involves the way people perceive and use time. Some cultures have a much more flexible concept of time than does mainstream American culture. This difference has given rise to stereotypical attitudes about productivity and efficiency. Americans work first, play later; some cultures, however, thread social interaction into the workday instead of putting it at the end. Their work gets done, but the pattern is different.

Formality

Another cultural variable is formality. In many cultures, formality is taken very seriously. As a marketing consultant, I have gone into many meetings with a senior executive of a company, greeted the individual using *Mr.* (occasionally *Ms.*), only to be told, "Call me Bob." By contrast, I will never forget the offended look on my Mexican client's face when a colleague of mine, in a misdirected attempt at friendship, called Guillermo (Spanish for William) Rodriguez Billy.

In selling or marketing to ethnics and minorities, it's a mistake to use a person's first name until and unless a relationship has been established. Many salespeople and telemarketers are trained to use prospects' first names to create rapport and establish an instantaneous relationship. African-Americans and others, however, are often offended when a white person, especially a white man, calls them by their first name, particularly if the white person uses a title and a last name to identify himself or herself. "That aversion dates from slavery when whites called all slaves by their first name, regardless of their respective age," says Noel A. Day, president of Polaris Research and Development of San Francisco.

Individualism

Individualism is another cultural issue. Mainstream American culture emphasizes the "I" consciousness, in which identity is rooted mostly in the self, compared to the "we" consciousness, in which a person's identity is rooted in groups. Latin American cultures and, to varying degrees, Asian cultures focus more on the group than on the individual.

For example, Chinese names place the family name before the given name; the Chinese name Wong Li Ping translates to Mr. Wong. Many Chinese-Americans, however, Anglicize the order of their names. Sometimes by the first generation, and certainly by the second and third generations, we see names such as Mr. Robert Wong.

More important, in Asian cultures it is inappropriate to call attention to oneself by what mainstream American culture calls blowing one's own horn. Americans may say, "The squeaky wheel gets the grease," but there is an expression in Japanese that says, "The nail that sticks up is the one that gets pounded down." When marketing to Japanese and Chinese consumers, it's a good idea not to show an individual achieving personal gain or performing a feat of heroism by using the product or service but to show how the family or group benefits from its use.

In Latin America, the group is the family or the extended family, and obligation to the family usually supersedes all other responsibilities. Because of the interlocking system of godparentship, families include both those who are blood relations and some who are not.

A few years ago, I rented a condominium in Puerto Rico and asked the housekeeper to buy a one-pound box of rice for the delicious Puerto Rican dish arroz con pollo (chicken with rice). She came back with a three-pound box of rice and apologized, explaining that there were no one-pound boxes.

My marketer's curiosity got the better of me, and I toured supermarkets within a twenty-mile radius of my condo. There were no one-pound boxes of rice to be found. Of course, I realized, rice is the primary staple of the island. Puerto Ricans tend to have large extended families, and members who drop in are always invited to have a plate of food. A one-pound box of rice would be gone in one dinner. Since the larger sizes are more economical, it's not unusual to see twenty- and fifty-pound sacks of rice at the big mainland-style supermarkets.

When designing packaging to appeal to the Hispanic market, cooking instructions and pictures should show culturally appropriate quantities. Also, when marketing to the Hispanic population, it's smart to avoid ads showing a diner eating alone; such ads would violate the well-known rule of marketing that people are most likely to buy products if they can identify with the individuals in the ads, promotion, or sales situation.

This family or group orientation was the key issue in the failure of a promotional campaign that was offered in Los Angeles, where there are a large number of Hispanics. Radio listeners were urged to enter a contest, with the prize of two expensive tickets to Disneyland. Promoters were astonished that so few people entered the contest. They failed to consider that many Hispanics have large or extended families and wouldn't think of participating in an offering in which they would have to choose only two members.

Rank, Hierarchy, and Tradition

The issues of rank, place, and hierarchy can affect buying patterns in the traditional Hispanic family. The head of the family is the "patron," or senior male, who is ultimately responsible for everyone in his family. To some degree, this arrangement limits the role of women in the family. Assimilation and acculturation have influenced this tradition, however, and in many Hispanic families buying decisions are now made by both husband and wife.

In traditional Latin American families, if a woman works, it implies that the men in the family cannot take care of her. Therefore, if you want to sell cars to first- or second-generation Hispanics, your advertising, promotion, and selling should have a group or family orientation.

Consider, for example, a 1990 ad campaign for a Chevrolet car in a mainstream women's magazine. The ad showed a pretty young woman saying, "What's the rush? Sure, I'd like to get married, but I love my work. And I don't have to answer to anybody."

This type of ad would not work well with Hispanic consumers, except, perhaps, for a third-generation, well-educated, highly assimilated woman of Hispanic ancestry in the Southwest. But softening the message by showing the young woman with friends or out driving with her husband and baby would key into the group or family identity that is so important to Hispanics.

Tradition is an important cultural value for many groups. Tradition plays a big role in the lives of Asian-Americans, who see change as not necessarily desirable. For many Asian-Americans, older is better. The elderly are revered for their knowledge and experience and are respected far more than young people.

Positioning a product as "new and improved," therefore, is not the best way to reach a traditional Asian consumer. A much better way to reach the Asian-American audience is to stress the manufacturer's long-standing reputation for quality and reliability: "We at XYZ Co. have produced quality products for thirty years and look forward to serving your family or company for years to come."

Preserving dignity and saving face are extremely important values for most Asians and many Hispanics. Knocking the competition in any selling campaign is frowned on, because the mud slinger causes the other company to lose face. It also makes the combative company look bad. Instead of comparing your products or services to those of the competition, emphasize the benefits and strengths of your own product or service.

Religion

Religion plays a big part in the way people perceive and use products and services. When George McGovern was campaigning for president in 1972, he offended traditionally observant Jews by visiting a kosher delicatessen and asking for a kosher hot dog and a glass of milk. Traditionally observant Jews are forbidden to mix dairy and meat products in the same cooking utensils or to eat them in the same meal. McGovern violated not only the kosher law but the marketers' law that reads, "Know thy product, know thy market." His gaffe clearly cost him many votes because negative word-of-mouth spreads like wildfire.

One U.S. company exported its goods to the Middle East with packaging that had stylized designs vaguely resembling crosses and stars on its packaging. In the Middle East, where Islam is the dominant religion, designs with what was interpreted to be Judeo-Christian symbols are unacceptable, and the company was booted out of the market.

Taste and Diet

Taste and diet play a big part in people's lives. Preferences are rooted partly in religion, partly in the practical question of what foods are available in a group's homeland.

It's easy to make mistakes if you're not tuned into these preferences. For example, some Asians are lactose-intolerant (as are some people of other ethnic groups). Most adults in China do not have dairy foods in their diets and consider cheese to be spoiled milk. Imagine their surprise, then, when a midwestern trade group visiting its sister city in China brought a wheel of (justifiably famous) cheese as a gift to its Chinese hosts.

A study reported in the May 1991 *Atlantic Monthly* magazine mapped areas of the United States where people are more likely than the average American to prefer tartness in their food and drink and areas where they are more likely to prefer sweetness. The map, which was based on market data about the popularity of lemon-lime soft drinks and which was called "The Lemon-Lime Latitudes," revealed that the areas where tart drinks don't sell well tend to have large proportions of black and Hispanic consumers and are clustered in the southern and coastal parts of the country. The article reported that "food historians say that popularity of sweets among blacks may have its roots, in part, in the plantation system of the South, where sugarcane was a source of cheap calories. Hispanic-American cuisine uses less meat and is more highly seasoned than northern European cuisine and demands a different complement; sweeter (or blander) flavors."

Colors, Numbers, and Symbols

Aesthetic elements, such as colors, numbers, symbols, and gestures, are important to consider when marketing to ethnics. If a foreign company were to use a black cat slinking through a ladder with thirteen rungs to illustrate the elegance or sleekness of its product, the ad probably wouldn't appeal to the many mainstream Americans who associate those symbols with bad luck.

Before you laugh at that image, consider that one U.S. company offered its products in Japan in lots of four displayed with white packaging. To many Asians, both the number four and white cloth or clothing are associated with death. To a mainstream American, on the other hand, the number four is quite innocuous and white is a symbol of purity.

Remember, too, when former President Ronald Reagan would get off an airplane somewhere in Latin America and give the A-OK sign, with his thumb and forefinger in a closed circle. To most Latin Americans (and to some Europeans and Asians), that gesture is obscene.

Assimilation and Acculturation

There are many cultural issues that may affect the marketing and sales success of your products and services. But we must also take into account the assimilation level of ethnic consumers in determining the marketing mix strategy for goods and services.

If we are doing our job properly, we'll take the time to research how assimilated our customers are. In addition to using geodemographic databases, we'll take a long look at where our ethnic and minority customers live and listen to how well they speak English.

We'll see what they eat and how they prepare it; find out how long they have lived in the United States; learn how and if their values have changed; see what their personal and professional affiliations are and what their education levels are. The level of assimilation and acculturation must be factored into marketing campaigns. (Assimilation is when an immigrant group adopts mainstream values and behaviors instead of keeping the culture of their heritage; acculturation means adding some elements of the mainstream culture without abandoning the native culture.) This may sound like a big job, but experience has shown that the gunshot method of marketing is more expensive in the long run, because it reaches few and alienates many.

It's interesting to note, however, that in marketing to teenagers and young adults, assimilation and acculturation sometimes work in reverse, that is, the mainstream takes on some aspects of the ethnic or minority culture. Black culture has strongly influenced the music, clothing, and speech of young people in the American mainstream and is considered quite fashionable.

In fact, this phenomenon has not only influenced U.S. teens but has given rise to a global "youth market." Just walk down any street in Tokyo, Munich, Lagos, Tel Aviv, Sao Paulo, or Chicago and, adjusting for regional ethnic differences, you'll see that teens look very much alike. They wear the same jeans, t-shirts, and sneakers, have similar hairstyles, eat and drink the same soda and burgers, and, most important, listen to the same pop music. Global goods, such as soda, jeans, cigarettes, and inexpensive cosmetics, can be sold in the same way with just about the same marketing campaign to any ethnic group anywhere in the world, thanks to the great pressure for conformity among teenagers, at least on the surface.

On the other end of the spectrum, expensive goods, such as diamonds, gold watches, luxury cars, and aged scotch, are also considered global goods and can be sold in much the same way to the very rich of almost any ethnic segment anywhere in the world. The people who regularly buy these goods have one important shared characteristic: money, and lots of it.

Once we move away from these two groups—one in which MTV has become its own subculture and one in which wealth is culturally unifying—we must consider the ways in which we differ in how we use and perceive things. Culture is a powerful and deep part of our lives. Marketers who hope to prosper in the twenty-first century will realize that tastes will never be uniform in the United States or anywhere else and will adapt their product line to reach profitable ethnic segments.

4

Marketing to Hispanics

A participant in a seminar I once gave asked, "What race are Hispanics?" I threw the question out to the group and wasn't surprised to hear many different answers—"black," "white," "brown," and "I don't know." The correct answer, of course, is "all of the above." Hispanic (or as some Americans of Spanish-speaking background prefer, Latino) refers to, not a race, but an origin or an ethnicity.*

Race is not a unifying factor for Hispanics; in fact, sometimes it is a divisive factor. It would be a mistake to pitch a product to a racially mixed Puerto Rican market by using only white Cuban models in a South Florida setting.

As the writer Enrique Fernandez observed, Puerto Ricans can be white, brown, or black; sometimes all three skin shades are found in the same family. Some Puerto Ricans think that the established white Cubans are snobbish and sarcastically call them "the creamy ones," referring to the color of their skin. But Dominicans, whose racial mix is more heavily African than that of Puerto Ricans, openly admire Cubans' economic success.

I saw ads recently for toothpaste and breakfast cereal on Spanish-language television in New York; both ads showed blonde children. This is a risky strategy. It may appeal to some viewers' aspirations but may alienate others. Here, as everywhere, the marketing rule is that people will buy a product they can identify with and feel good about.

*For the sake of convenience, most of the time I use the word *Hispanic*, which is the designation used by the U.S. Census Bureau.

Hispanics—One Market or Many?

There is no one monolithic "Hispanic market"—only a group of Hispanic segments. Although the overall strategy for marketing to Hispanics can be standardized, the advertising usually cannot. Occasionally, however, well-designed research and test marketing show that a product is a "universal" for the Hispanic market, that it is perceived, used, and purchased in the same way by Cubans, Puerto Ricans, and Mexicans. In these cases a cost-efficient, standardized pan-Hispanic promotional campaign may be what's needed.

What, if anything, unifies Hispanics? For the most part, the Spanish language and Catholicism. But even here, the market is not homogeneous because of bilingualism, assimilation, and changing religious patterns. Although the overwhelming majority of Spanish-speaking people throughout the world are still Roman Catholics, evangelical Protestantism is now the fastest-growing religion in Latin America and among Hispanics in the United States. Hispanics are also followers of other Christian denominations, Judaism, and African-influenced and Native American religions.

Even among Spanish-speaking Catholics, the Hispanic market is not monolithic. There are demographic, geographic, and psychographic differences to be taken into account. Combine these variations with differences in the degree of assimilation and acculturation and you get a market that is highly segmented. For the most part, mainstream marketers haven't yet segmented Hispanics beyond the mass market stage.

National Origin

The single most important segmentation factor among Hispanics is the country of national origin. The culture, beliefs, opinions, and, most important, consumer behavior patterns of Cuban-Americans, Mexican-Americans, Puerto Ricans, Dominicans, Salvadorans, and other Hispanics are not identical, a result of the influence of differences in their native countries' geography, indigenous ancestry, colonial origins, and climate.

Even among immigrant groups from the same country, there are significant cultural variations arising from differences in education, degree of assimilation, and socioeconomic status.

Immigrants from large countries, such as Mexico, may exhibit cultural differences based on the region of the country from which they come (just as there are differences among customs in different regions of the United States). For example, the fun-loving, relatively unsophisticated Mexicans from Veracruz, an East Coast port city on the Gulf of Mexico, are quite different from the highly sophisticated, entrepreneurial Mexicans from Monterrey, which is only a three-hour drive from the Texas border.

Cubans' culture differs radically from that of the Mexicans. There is a large cultural gap between the wealthy landowners and professionals who fled from Fidel Castro's Cuba in 1959–1960 and the poorer Marielitos who were ejected from Cuba, some coming directly from Cuban jails, and who landed in the United States in 1980.

These differences shouldn't surprise marketers who have segmented and subsegmented mainstream America into thousands of micromarkets. Yet when I speak to marketing executives, individually or at seminars, I am often met with skepticism or, worse, an exhausted sigh at the thought of being burdened with more work. Of course, it's more work to segment Hispanics, but the payback is capturing a market that is the fastest growing in the United States.

Unifying Factors

Although the $200 billion Hispanic market is not a monolith, several values serve to unite Hispanics. They include the importance placed on the family and children, the desire to preserve their ethnicity, an emphasis on aesthetics and emotions, a devotion to religion and tradition, and a strong interest in their appearance. Another unifying factor is the emphasis on quality of life and enjoyment.

There is a popular saying in Mexico that "one works to live, not lives to work." Hispanics do not focus solely on task achievement, as do many mainstream Americans, but emphasize taking pleasure in the process, whether the process of work or overall lifestyle. The Puritan work ethic dominant in America motivates mainstream Anglos to work the day long; *then* when you are finished you can relax and have fun. Hispanics attempt to thread some pleasure throughout the long, difficult workday. This cultural difference has given rise to the unpleasant and incorrect stereotype of the unmotivated Hispanic. The stereotype is based on the fact that Hispanics' time frames don't always conform to those of the mainstream. It's easy to see how such misunderstandings can create cultural clashes and worse.

In marketing to Hispanics, try to focus on these unifying cultural factors. An awareness of the differences between Hispanic subsegments is important, but it's even more important to concentrate on the things that Hispanics have in common.

Hispanic Migration

People migrate to the United States for a variety of reasons, not the least of which is that, with all its problems, the United States is the most open country in the world politically, economically, and philosophically. It's still one of the only places in the world where a poor kid can become president—of the country or of General Motors. If I had been born almost anywhere else and were still living there, I'd still be poor as I was as a child. Most places in the world do not permit changes in rank and status. Because I was able to educate myself, I have pulled myself up by my bootstraps to a comfortable lifestyle.

Hispanics come to the United States for the same economic, political, and social opportunities that attract other immigrants to America. The largest group of Hispanics in the United States—close to 13 million people—comes from Mexico. Mexican-Americans live primarily in the southwestern states of California and Texas, but since the 1980s large numbers of Mexicans have been migrating to northeastern states, including New York and Massachusetts.

Americans of Puerto Rican descent account for more than

2.5 million people in the United States. They live primarily in New York, New Jersey, and Chicago. The Census Bureau in 1990 counted close to 500,000 people from the Dominican Republic, most of whom live in New York and New Jersey, but it is widely acknowledged that the real number is higher, because many Dominicans are undocumented and evaded census takers.

Central and South Americans account for more than 2.2 million people in the United States. They are the fastest growing group of Hispanics in the United States.

Cubans, concentrated in Florida, with some scattered in the Northeast, account for slightly more than 1 million people, and Spanish and "other" unclassified Hispanics account for another 1.6 million people. Remember that these are all official Census Bureau numbers; officials acknowledge that Hispanics were undercounted by more than 10 percent because many Hispanics are undocumented and won't disclose their status to the government.

The Census Bureau projects that there will be more than 30 million Hispanics by 2000 and more than 40 million by 2010. The growth rate for the Hispanic population is four to five times that for the U.S. population as a whole.

Hispanic families tend to be larger than those of mainstream Americans, and the average age of Hispanics is seven years younger than the average for the general population. From a marketer's point of view, this segment represents a very rich lode, in contrast to the mainstream market, which is growing very slowly, if at all. Yet the Hispanic segment, which makes up more than 10 percent of the U.S. population, has been neglected by most marketers and advertisers.

Traditions and Identity

All statistics and research project continued growth in the Hispanic market and foresee its continued adherence to its traditions and its identity, the result of increased immigration, retro-acculturation, and Hispanics' efforts to maintain their cultural values. Many young acculturated and assimilated Hispanics, for example, speak Spanish at home even though they are fluent in English and English is their dominant language.

According to the Latino National Political Survey, conducted in 1992 by Professor Rodolfo O. de la Garza of the University of Texas at Austin, a large majority of the Hispanics born in the United States speak English better than Spanish, and English literacy is high even among foreign-born Hispanics who prefer to speak Spanish. Nonetheless, most Hispanics want their children to know Spanish and to take pride in their cultural heritage. Not only do parents want their children to be proud of their background; the children are vigorously asserting their pride. The actor Martin Sheen found that his Spanish name, Ramon Estevez, severely limited his range as a young actor in the early 1960s. In contrast, one of his actor sons, fair, blue-eyed Emilio Estevez, who came of cinematic age in the mid-1980s, proudly uses his real name, yet he has not been typecast, nor has his range been limited by anything other than his ability.

Speaking Their Language

How do we reach the almost 25 million Hispanics in the United States today? By understanding the similarities and differences among the segments, by designing and selling goods and services that are appropriate to these segments, and by advertising and promoting products in ways that "speak" their language.

A survey done by Katz Hispanic Radio Research in New York reported that 87 percent of all Hispanic adults described themselves as "very Hispanic." The numbers varied by region; in the Northeast, 90 percent did so; in the Southeast and in the central United States, 88 percent; in the West, 89 percent; and in the Southwest, 68 percent. The Southwest has the oldest, most established, and probably most assimilated Hispanic population in the United States.

The Katz survey noted that the three main categories of Hispanic assimilation patterns pointed out the benefits of using Spanish language ads: 9.7 percent of U.S. Hispanics are totally assimilated and reached via general market media; 41.4 percent of U.S. Hispanic adults are partially assimilated and prefer Spanish-language media; and 49.2 percent of U.S. Hispanics are unassimilated, do not speak English, and are reached exclusively by Spanish-language media.

Hispanic Media

There's a category of Spanish media for every type of individual. In 1992 the Hispanic edition of Standard Rate and Data Service listed forty-two major Spanish-language magazines, thirty-one English or bilingual Hispanic-oriented magazines, and 103 Spanish-language newspapers in the United States. The acknowledged leaders in the Spanish-language magazine category are *Mas* and *Una Nueva Vida*; there are specialized magazines, from *Cosmo* (*Cosmopolitan* in Spanish) to the high-circulation English-language *Hispanic Business* to the well-regarded magazine supplement *Vista*, distributed to many newspapers.

An estimated 80 percent of Hispanics listen to the four national Hispanic radio networks and the more than three hundred stations with Spanish-language programming. Only 16 percent listen to primarily English-language radio.

Most Hispanic advertising dollars go to Spanish television, which is watched by more than three-quarters of Hispanic households. Hispanics spend 26 percent more time than does the general market watching television, especially the Univision and Telemundo Broadcast networks and the Galavision cable network. In 1993 MTV launched a Miami-based Spanish network targeting twelve-to-thirty-four-year-old Hispanics.

In general, Hispanics are more likely to prefer ads in which the information is presented in Spanish. They pay more attention to these ads and are more likely to recall them.

Most Hispanics are highly brand-conscious and loyal to companies that advertise in Spanish. Roberto Orci, senior vice president of La Agencia de Orci y Asociados, a Los Angeles ad agency, explains that marketers can prove that Hispanics watch

English-language television. "But they don't watch the commercials. They feel that for them to listen to an English-language commercial, they have to work two to three times as hard to understand it. When they finally understand it, they say, 'It's not for me!' "

"If you want to talk to my heart, talk to me in Spanish," says the fully bilingual Mr. Orci. Simply put, dollars invested in targeted advertising aimed at Hispanics generate a higher rate of return than dollars invested in mainstream media.

This finding conflicts with Linda Chavez's assertion, in a *Forbes* magazine article that appeared in March 1992, that by the third generation most Hispanics speak English only, as she does. With her university degrees and her stint as staff director of the U.S. Civil Rights Commission in the Reagan administration, however, Ms. Chavez is hardly representative of the majority of Hispanics. Chavez's article, and a December 1991 *Forbes* article that asserted that Hispanics prefer English-language to Spanish-language television, is precisely the kind of misinformation that "fuels advertisers' skepticism about this and other ethnic markets," says Dr. Gonzalo R. Soruco, professor of advertising at the University of Miami's School of Communications. But Dr. Soruco argues that the heart of the problem lies in the lack of accurate, standardized market research and the very complex Hispanic market and its segments.

Understanding Hispanic Culture

The important thing to remember when seeking to target the fertile Hispanic consumer market is that you must look carefully at all the indicators and then research, analyze, and segment.

Just how important are cultural issues and how different are Hispanics from the mainstream? The Mexican poet and essayist Octavio Paz described his understanding: "In the [U.S.] ethic, the center is the individual; in Hispanic morals, the true protagonist is the family."

Compared to their counterparts in the general market,

U.S. Hispanics tend to be more committed to traditional middle-class values. According to Isabel Valdes, president of Hispanic Market Connections in Los Altos, California, "the lifestyle process is different for Hispanics and mainstream America. Hispanic children stay closer to their mother, who give out affection much longer. Education could take longer for the traditional Hispanic consumer, and therefore adolescence may be shorter."

Key rites of passage may be celebrated differently in Hispanic culture. For example, the traditional sweet sixteen party for girls becomes the *quinceañera,* or the celebration of a girl's coming of age at fifteen. If you develop a commercial that doesn't reflect a Hispanic's expectation of the life-cycle event, the viewer will say, "Obviously this ad is not for me; it was done for another group." One way to bridge this gap is to design an ad that will appeal to the mainstream but still contain a message relevant to Hispanics.

For a McDonald's commercial, Ferrar/Ad America, a Los Angeles agency, pictured a celebration that looked like a simple birthday party to most viewers. But Hispanics knew it was a *quinceañera.* And although Hispanics as a group make less money than mainstream consumers, they spend proportionally the same as the general market for video cameras, cameras, and goods that are geared to family occasions.

J. C. Penney has also targeted the *quinceañeras* as an important part of its Hispanic marketing campaign. Taking note of *quinceañeras* is only one small part of the J. C. Penney approach; the company shows great sensitivity to Hispanic (as well as to African-American) culture and family values.

Most of Penney's television spots use a story line dealing with Hispanic family life and show four or five products during the scenario, a "soft sell" that puts the merchandise in a cultural context. By demonstrating its sensitivity to a group that places tremendous importance on family and ethnic occasions, holidays, and festivals, Penney differentiates itself from other mass marketers.

Family Values and Marketing

Courtship tends to last somewhat longer for Hispanics than for mainstream Americans. Being romantic is very important to the culture, and parents and family are involved in courtship rituals. Divorce is still unacceptable for most Hispanics, who tend to stay married for life. (However, with increasing assimilation, there has been a growing acceptance of divorce and remarriage.)

The importance of the family and children, even to the assimilated Hispanic consumer, shouldn't be underestimated. The ideal is a large family, which includes a system of godparentship (in Spanish, *compadrazgo*), in which godmothers and godfathers are considered part of the extended family. The family is the center of everything, and everyone participates in the holidays, rituals, and festivals.

Mainstream America may have rejected the idea of the meddling mother-in-law, but a recent ad on Spanish-language television showed a young couple nervously awaiting his mother's approval of his bride's cooking. (No one is suggesting, of course, that using this somewhat stereotypical formula will bring success to every mainstream marketer who tries to win Hispanic customers.) But let's find out what *is* important to the Hispanic segments when selling our goods and services.

Hispanics tend to have larger families than the U.S. average, with almost 3.5 people per household compared to the national average of just over 2.5. Hispanic families spend considerably more of their income on groceries than does the general market. Not only does the immediate family gathers for dinner; people in the extended family often join in, making the meal a social event.

Most Hispanics consider their obligations to their extended family extremely important. The ideal of devotion was illustrated in a fascinating find by the 1986 University of Arizona Garbage Project, funded by Heinz, U.S.A. During the course of the study, those people who had their garbage analyzed were asked if they had used any prepared baby foods over the past week. Although not one of the Hispanic mothers admitted to using even one jar of baby food, the garbage from the Hispanic households had just as many baby food jars as did garbage from other households with infants. Although almost half of the Hispanic women in the neighborhood were in the workforce, they still reported clinging to the idealized cultural expectation that a mother will devote all her time to caring for the family.

Because few people behave in the way they report to researchers, we see once again a need to use observational research, along with culturally relevant focus groups, question-naires, samples, and surveys, to learn about our target populations.

Food companies should alway emphasize taste when marketing to Hispanics. Delicious meals that please the senses are the ideal, while mentioning the fat content would be seen by many Hispanics as denying the pleasure. Hispanics, like everyone else today, are concerned with fat and cholesterol. But when advertising a cooking oil, or any food for that matter, taste and flavor should always be the primary benefit.

The elders in Hispanic families are shown the utmost respect, since in the Hispanic tradition, age means acquired experience and knowledge. Change and innovation are not always considered as desirable as they are in the mainstream culture.

Gender roles, as I noted in Chapter 3, are more strictly adhered to in Hispanic homes than they are in mainstream America. Today, however, Hispanic men and women say major product and lifestyle decisions are being made jointly, except for the older generation and in newly arrived immigrant families. Families tend to view shopping as an occasion or outing and frequently shop together.

More on Assimilation and Acculturation

Although 33 percent of U.S.-born Hispanics marry Anglos, close to 80 percent of *all* Hispanics marry Hispanics, so there is fairly slow acculturation and assimilation into the mainstream. Educated Hispanics acculturate faster, but as a rule research shows that acculturation of most Hispanic immigrants often takes up to four generations. Even upwardly mobile, acculturated Hispanics usually don't fully adopt mainstream values; in terms of core values, the assimilation process is extremely slow.

As a result, there is, in some Hispanic subsegments, little

difference between first- and second-generation Hispanics. Younger Hispanics, however, may be more comfortable with English than are older Hispanics. One interesting language quirk, observed among U.S.-born Hispanics, is the practice of slipping back and forth between English and Spanish, with part of a sentence in English and part in Spanish.

Second- and third-generation Hispanics sometimes Anglicize the pronunciation of their names. At a sales training program I gave recently, one of the participants was listed on the roster as Jack Echavarria. When I called the roster, I said "Etch-ah-vah-REE-ah" in the traditional Spanish pronunciation. He gently corrected me and said, "it's pronounced "Etch-uh-VAR-ee-uh," conforming to the rules of English pronunciation. Jack, who was born on the U.S. mainland to Puerto Rican-born parents, felt he would have more mobility in the mainstream business world if he used the English pronunciation.

The Hybrid Market

According to Henry Adams-Esquivel, vice president of MDI in San Diego, the melting-pot effect is not usually evident in the Hispanic population. Although Hispanics who have been in the United States for a long period of time are typically bilingual, they do not become Americanized or assimilated. Instead, a third possibility—a "hybrid market"—is created out of attitudes that are neither completely Hispanic nor American but a combination of the two.

To illustrate this hybrid market, consider the area of food. The first generation of Hispanics often clings to its native eating customs, and the children may eat "Hispanic" food at home. But second-generation Hispanics, especially teenagers, often discard the ethnic tradition and assert their Americanness by eating American foods out of the home. This may be more the result of the global youth market, with its pressure for surface conformity, than of any deep structural changes. On the other hand, it may be an example of how one successful Hispanic executive defines acculturation. Having lived in the United States for twenty-five years, he feels acculturated but not assimilated. He says, "Acculturation is the process whereby a minority or immigrant group adopts some of the characteristics of another culture without replacing their own."

The rates of acculturation and assimilation vary for different aspects of people's lives. Acculturation may involve only surface behavior, conformity with the observable values of mainstream culture. For example, for most poor people around the world, one symbol of wealth is being fat. It shows the world that you have plenty of money with which to eat and feed your family. However, in the United States, it is considered a sign of prosperity to be slim. As one socialite put it some years ago, "A woman can never be too thin or too rich." Judging from the time and money spent on diet preparations, most mainstream Americans have bought into this thinking. And, by the third generation, many Hispanics in the United States are spending a good deal of money on dieting and fitness regimens.

Patterns of assimilation differ among different groups of Hispanics. According to the Miami-based Strategy Research Corporation, "Cubans report feeling less assimilated than any other Hispanic group in the U.S." Although they may have been in the United States for many years and may have achieved tremendous economic and political success, many Cubans feel that they are Cuban only and will someday return to Cuba.

Mexican-Americans report feeling most assimilated, with almost two-thirds feeling either highly or partially assimilated. But when asked to describe how Hispanic- or Latin-oriented they would like to be in the future, 83 percent report that they would like to be "very Hispanic."

There is no question that a fairly large number of Hispanics are acculturating and, to varying degrees, assimilating. But this fact doesn't lessen the importance of attempting to reach the various geodemographic segments of the market with products and services developed and promoted in a culturally appropriate fashion.

Listen to Isabel Valdes: "Mexican families tend to preserve identifiable aspects of their culture in many aspects of life for many generations." Even affluent Mexican-Americans who are educated and acculturated may not have assimilated in the full sense of adopting all American values.

I recently spent time with a Mexican-American family consisting of a second-generation father, a second-generation mother, and their third-generation teenage son. The father is a senior executive in a mainstream job, the mother is a fortyish part-time worker and homemaker. They are affluent and live in an upscale suburb of Los Angeles. In every way, they mirror the typical mainstream family and are the embodiment of the American dream.

However, although they are acculturated almost to the point of assimilation, they retain much of their culture. And like most Hispanics, they take pride in that culture. On one occasion, when they took my husband and me to dinner, they drove past many chic little restaurants and took us to a traditional Mexican eatery, where they proudly ordered for us in Spanish. Another time, they hosted a dinner party for a group that included some of the husband's important business contacts and served only Mexican food.

From a marketer's point of view, highly acculturated Hispanics may seem demographically similar to the mainstream, but they are keenly aware and highly appreciative of any effort made by a marketing campaign or promotional mix that acknowledges their considerable purchasing power. They look beyond a product when they buy something; 40 percent of Hispanics say they prefer to buy products from companies that show an interest in the Hispanic consumer.

The Southwest

If southern California is the heart of the most dynamic Mexican-American market in the United States, the southwestern states have the most established, acculturated, and assimilated Hispanic communities. San Antonio, designated an "All-American City," is probably the most established Mexican city on this side of the Rio Grande. Henry Cisneros, secretary of housing and urban development in the Clinton administration, was formerly the mayor of San Antonio and was the first Hispanic mayor of a major U.S. city.

In San Antonio, although everyone speaks English (along with Spanish) and is highly acculturated, not everyone is totally assimilated. The culture is Mexican *and* American, two cultures coexisting, with no need to deny either. This type of long-standing dual market has also developed in other cities in Texas, New Mexico, Arizona, and Colorado. Consumers in these cities respond to goods and services that recognize their dual heritage. They celebrate Cinco de Mayo and also the Fourth of July.

Mexican-Americans

More than 42 percent of affluent Hispanics, the majority Mexican-Americans, live in the West. These well-to-do Hispanics, earning more than $50,000 a year, make up one of the fastest growing market segments.

There is also a growing number of poor Mexican families like that pictured on the infamous CAUTION! sign a few miles south of San Diego. This sign shows a silhouette of two running adults and a child running behind. They are dashing across the six lanes of Highway 5 to leave Mexico behind in search of work in the United States. Like a deer-crossing sign in other parts of the nation, people here have become a driver's hazard.

Many Mexicans are so determined to get to the United States that they take tremendous risks crossing the border, and they often take any job they can get once they make it. Mexican-Americans make up close to 65 percent of U.S. Hispanics, and their numbers have increased by almost 55 percent since 1980, a much faster rate of increase than the rate for Puerto Ricans or Cubans. Mexicans are the youngest Hispanic subgroup.

This huge Mexican market is highly motivated. Look at the Lynwood neighborhood of Los Angeles, which is officially poorer even than its next-door neighbor Watts. There are shops, banks, motels, and people reading Spanish-language newspapers, buying food from street vendors, and setting up neighborhood institutions that mirror those they left behind. But there is a big difference in Los Angeles—the opportunity to thrive. Even these, the poorest consumers, do just that— consume. This market is likely to continue to experience tremendous growth.

A *Newsweek* article has suggested that a "reconquista," or reconquest, of formerly Mexican territories is taking place. Whatever the interpretation, this market will dominate southern California in the twenty-first century, and smart marketers will reach these consumers within the context of their cultural background.

In 1991 McDonald's celebrated Cinco de Mayo (the Fifth of May), a Mexican national holiday commemorating Mexico's victory over the French in 1862, by adding chicken fajitas, a popular Mexican dish, to the menu. The target at first was Mexican-Americans in the West and Southwest, but the product was a great hit with the mainstream, as well. Fajitas (chronically mispronounced) can now be found not only at McDonald's but on menus practically all over the United States, with the possible exception (only temporarily) of Greek diners in New York.

Puerto Ricans

Puerto Rico, a tiny island with few natural resources, lies across the Mona Channel from the Dominican Republic. It has been a commonwealth of the United States since 1917. Puerto Ricans began emigrating to New York in large numbers in the 1940s, usually settling in poor and black neighborhoods. Migration broke up families, and some Puerto Ricans assimilated with the dominant black culture of the neighborhoods. Over the years, many Puerto Ricans prospered and moved to other places; some went back to Puerto Rico.

Half of all Puerto Rican immigrants to the United States settle in New York. Except for a highly educated professional group, those who stay in New York permanently seem to do worse economically than those who settle in other parts of the country. In the past few years, many college-educated Puerto Ricans have settled in the Sun Belt states.

I once spent some time talking to owners of small shops in Puerto Rico and found that many of them had lived for a time in New York, New Jersey, or Philadelphia. They had worked hard, saved carefully, and returned to Puerto Rico as shop owners instead of retiring.

In a study done by Strategy Research Corporation of Miami on the assimilation of Puerto Ricans, fewer than 10 percent of those questioned said they felt highly assimilated. Even though Puerto Ricans have been entitled to U.S. citizenship since 1917 and can move freely between Puerto Rico and the mainland, many feel that their home is Puerto Rico. As with Cubans, this desire to return seems to reduce Puerto Ricans' interest in assimilating.

Like most Hispanics, Puerto Ricans are very warm and sociable people. They respond to people and things that reflect similar warmth and sociability, including ads that appeal to their upbeat personalities. Advertisers need to demonstrate a sense of warmth in their promotions to Puerto Ricans, perhaps more than with other Hispanic groups. Puerto Ricans are also pretty sophisticated consumers, having been exposed to mainland goods and services both on the island and the mainland.

Dominicans

The established bloc of Puerto Ricans in the New York/New Jersey metropolitan area is being joined by newer immigrants from the Dominican Republic. Although a few Dominicans live in New Jersey and in the Miami metropolitan area, most seem to settle near the Puerto Rican communities of the North, rather than the Cuban ones in South Florida. According to Enrique Fernandez, writing in New York's *Village Voice*, "Dominicans tend not to settle near Cubans because of discrimination against the majority of Dominicans who are black and varying shades of brown."

The Dominican Republic shares the island of Hispaniola with French-speaking Haiti, the first black republic in the

Americas. The country has had its share of political upheaval; although the U.S. Marines have been called in to keep the calm during two difficult periods of civil strife, most Dominicans have very positive feelings toward the United States.

Dominicans in New York, although they have many traits in common with Puerto Ricans, do not usually assimilate into the Puerto Rican community. (In recent years, however, there has been an increase in the number of Dominican-Puerto Rican marriages.)

Undocumented Dominicans often arrive in the United States via boat passage from the Dominican Republic to Puerto Rico, followed by a domestic flight to the mainland. Because Puerto Ricans do not have to pass through immigration, it's fairly easy for undocumented Dominicans to enter the United States in this way and rather difficult for immigration officials to pick them out of a crowd of Puerto Ricans who are legally entering the mainland.

The official 1990 census counted about half a million Dominicans in the continental United States, but unofficial estimates suggest there may be more than 1 million Dominicans in New York alone. Undocumented Dominicans don't qualify for public assistance and often take low-paying jobs or work for entrepreneurial relatives who have already become established.

Dominicans make up close to 40 percent of New York's Hispanics and own almost 70 percent of Hispanic small businesses. Half of the 167 supermarkets in New York's C-Town chain are Dominican-owned, as are all 36 of the new Bravo supermarkets. Most of these supermarkets are in fairly tough neighborhoods where major chains have either pulled out or never entered.

Adversity, the Dominicans say, helps them stand together, and they go out of their way to help each other. Dominicans tend to move out of Manhattan to the outer boroughs of New York City or to New Jersey when they have saved enough money.

Cuban-Americans

Although a fair number of Cubans have lived in the New Jersey metropolitan area since the 1960s, the vast majority of Cuban-

Americans live in South Florida, primarily in and around Miami and Tampa. Cuba is a huge island with great natural resources, located just ninety miles from the U.S. mainland. In the years leading up to Fidel Castro's overthrow of the Battista government, the island was considered a hotbed of corruption. Once the communists took over in 1959, those professionals and business owners who could leave did so quickly, because Castro nationalized all businesses for the "good of the revolution."

When the Cubans settled in Miami, they transformed decaying areas of the city and boosted the local economy, making the city an international center some call "the capital of Latin America." Xavier Suarez, a former mayor of Miami, was the first Cuban-born mayor of any major U.S. city. Alberto Alvarez, president of the Miami-based AmeriSecurities Capital Corporation, believes that Miami is becoming the main Latin financial center. His company and others make Miami a magnet for Latin Americans. Look at his employees; all fifteen of them are of Latin descent; they were all born in Cuba, Nicaragua, Peru, Guatemala, or Puerto Rico.

Cubans are the most affluent Hispanic subgroup, with a median household income almost $10,000 higher than that of Puerto Ricans. Some of that difference may be the result of the Cuban-Americans' median age of almost forty years, much higher than that of other Hispanics and even higher than the U.S. median age. Older usually means more experience in the workforce and higher pay resulting from seniority.

Adding to the advantage of age is education. Close to 20 percent of all Cubans over twenty-five have completed four years of college, compared to 10 percent of Puerto Ricans and 6 percent of Mexican-Americans.

Many people wonder if the Cubans will return to Cuba when Fidel Castro either dies or relinquishes his power. If a significant number of Cuban-Americans were to go to Cuba (which I doubt), Miami and other cities would lose not only part of their tax base but also an important part of the U.S. Hispanic community. In fact, of course, it's been almost thirty-five years since the first emigrants left Cuba, and many Cuban-Americans have no idea what Cuba looks like. (For those who want a taste of the old country, pre-Castro Cuba lives on in Miami's Little Havana, on streets like Calle Ocho.)

"Walter Cronkite" Spanish

The advertising industry is still somewhat divided over the issue of using standard, nonregional "Walter Cronkite" Spanish. Even if Hispanics design a campaign, there's no guarantee that they're familiar with all the ways that words are used by different Hispanic groups. According to Julia Lieblich, writing in *Fortune* magazine, "the word 'bichos,' for example, means bugs to Mexicans. To Puerto Ricans, it means a man's private parts. An insecticide company's posters guaranteed to kill all 'bichos' left executives blushing." However, standard Spanish presented in an informal style usually succeeds.

Part of this successful approach is choosing the right word when there are regional alternatives. The University of Chicago Spanish dictionary lists a large number of regional translations for *little boy*. In Mexico, it's *chamoco*; in Guatemala, *patojo*; in El Salvador, *cipote*; in Cuba, *chico*. In Puerto Rico, a little boy is called *nino* (or its slang form, *nene*), and in the Dominican Republic, "muchacho." In a national pan-Hispanic rollout, however, most U.S. Hispanics would understand "nino" or "muchacho."

National, Regional, or Local?

The question then remains whether a national campaign is more or less effective than a local or a regional one. One example of a successful regional approach was the Coca-Cola ad campaign in which the company regionalized its ads, tailoring them for Hispanic segments in the Northeast, the Southeast, and the West and the Southwest.

The ads featured the Coke logo and a can of the soda, along with the words "y su comida favorita" ("and your favorite meal"), shown with arroz con pollo (chicken and rice) for the northeastern Puerto Rican segment, traditional pork loin for the southeastern Cuban-American segment, and a dish of tacos for the Mexican-American segments in the West and the Southwest.

I have found that regionalized campaigns are more cost-efficient than local or national campaigns for many products and services but that only certain products can be advertised using a regional strategy.

Whether national, regional, or local, one thing is certain: Not enough marketers are spending the time and the money to capture the Hispanic market. And the outlay doesn't have to be great. It costs far less to reach Hispanic consumers than to reach mainstream consumers, because Hispanic media costs are lower than those for media reaching the general market.

Appealing to Hispanic Consumers

What is needed for a successful Hispanic promotional campaign is a sensitivity to what is important to Hispanics.

Hispanic communities are very tightly knit, and the interlocking families and relationships provide a ready network for word-of-mouth promotion. While advertising at the local or regional level is very important, sponsorships, contests, sweepstakes and lotteries, and event marketing can be more powerful tools in the promotional mix.

Coupons have a negative connotation for some Hispanics, particularly Puerto Rican consumers, since they may be perceived as similar to food stamps. One study found that coupon usage for inner-city Puerto Rican consumers averaged only about 30 percent; the usage rate soared to 80 percent for Mexican-Americans in the Southwest.

One successful promotion that involved coupons was run by Great Events Promotion of Great Neck, New York, which organized "Festival Latino," combining coupon savings with a sweepstakes package. When customers used the coupons, they automatically became registered in the sweepstakes and were eligible to win cars, trips, televisions, and other expensive prizes.

In general, event marketing is a good way to reach the

Hispanic consumer. Sponsoring sporting events, music festivals, parades, and religious holiday celebrations and supporting educational organizations provides good exposure for advertisers.

In 1992 most marketers missed the opportunity presented by the celebration of the five hundredth anniversary of the arrival of Columbus in the New World. Columbus, even though he was Italian, is important to most Hispanics and has particular significance for Dominicans, since he is believed to have first set foot in the New World on their island in 1492. In a survey of Hispanic consumers conducted for *Marketing News*, approximately 70 percent said that Columbus is a beloved figure in the Hispanic community. Companies would be well advised not to wait until the six hundredth anniversary of Columbus's arrival in 2092 to find opportunities to reach out to this market.

Many first-generation Hispanics, like other immigrant groups, don't look outside their community for financial help in establishing or operating a business. In general, Hispanics have remained fairly self-contained, often banding together in associations such as the Hispanic Chambers of Commerce. Any company that is interested in successfully marketing to a Hispanic community should get involved for the long term with these groups or similar organizations, such as church groups and educational/benevolent associations. The *Hispanic Resource Directory 1992–1994*, edited by Alan Schorr, lists 6,200 Hispanic organizations and associations in the United States.

Financial Services

Only a handful of mainstream companies go after the savings, investment, and insurance business of the Hispanic market. In the general market, one household in four invests in mutual funds, but only one in fifty Hispanic households invests in such funds.

According to the Census Bureau, in 1990 28 percent of Hispanics in the United States lacked health insurance, compared to 12 percent of whites and 18 percent of blacks. Insurance is too expensive for many Hispanics, but it's possible that insurance providers haven't made much of an effort to target the Hispanic market.

Life insurance is expensive, too, but New York's Metropolitan Life Insurance Company increased sales of insurance to Hispanics by more than 150 percent by using nationwide ad campaigns. The company also placed Hispanic sales representatives in its seven largest Hispanic markets and provided well-translated promotional literature.

In its multimedia campaign, Met Life referred to the importance of the family and the need to protect its future. When selling to Hispanics, it's usually a good idea to evoke a positive vision of the family; if it's done with emotion and eloquence, so much the better.

Frank Cruz, the head of Gulf Atlantic Life Insurance Company in Los Angeles, says that his company's ads are geared to Hispanics' strong family orientation. His company has been especially successful in advertising to recent immigrants by using the nine Spanish-language radio stations in the Los Angeles area.

In New York and Miami, banks have been springing up to serve the Spanish-speaking population. Often, they replace money-center banks, which have reduced their presence in poorer urban areas. These banks hope to capture savings and to recycle some of the money to the Hispanic communities.

Golden Opportunities for Marketers

Financial services isn't the only category in which the opportunities for selling to Hispanics haven't been fully tapped. Many Hispanics show a strong preference for cars made by the "Big Three" U.S. automakers (General Motors, Ford, and Chrysler). Yet according to Isabel Valdes, Honda was the top-selling car to Hispanics for at least two years running. "Honda sought out the Hispanic market and targeted ads to them," she says. At a time when mainstream America continues its love affair with imports, Detroit cannot afford to ignore this potential market.

Ms. Valdes also suggests that Hispanic women and the

Hispanic youth market are not being targeted adequately by mainstream marketers. Hispanic women, she says, outspend the general market on their children and are dependent on Spanish-language promotion. Equally underrepresented in Hispanic media are ads for the host of educational products and services that Hispanics are hungry for—everything from books, computer and technical training, and language courses to colleges and universities. One company that has capitalized on this unmet need is the Encyclopedia Britannica, which has had a good deal of success with its Spanish-language edition.

Good grooming and an attractive appearance are important values for Hispanics. Hispanics buy cosmetics and toiletries at a far higher rate than does mainstream America. In recent years, many manufacturers of cosmetics, toiletries, and fashionable clothing have begun targeting African-American consumers; few of these companies have made the effort to reach the Hispanic market. When a company does make this effort, as Avon did, the response is overwhelming, as Sonia Green of Avon reports at the end of this chapter.

While mainstream consumers are bombarded by direct-mail campaigns for every type of merchandise and service, Hispanics receive only about 30 percent as many direct-mail solicitations as general-market consumers. If the objectives of direct mail are to create awareness and to educate the consumer, some companies are missing out on a good opportunity. Many people in the mainstream are so overloaded by unsolicited direct mail that they throw most of it away without reading it. The general market for direct mail is saturated, but the Hispanic market for direct mail is still in its infancy.

Some suggest that soliciting catalog purchases from Hispanics is a waste of time because Hispanics prefer shopping in person. Although Hispanics clearly prefer personal shopping, many Hispanic households whose members are hard-pressed for time would surely welcome catalog shopping.

Brand Loyalty

When Hispanics are happy with the products and services they consume, they are likely to stay with them. Hispanics tend to be somewhat more brand-loyal than mainstream consumers, especially if a company remains sensitive to Hispanic needs.

About 45 percent of Hispanics always buy their usual brands, whereas about only 20 to 25 percent switch brands frequently. Marketers have offered many reasons for this brand consciousness, including lack of exposure to a market full of competitors, a wish to buy prestige goods from a market leader, and a desire to do the best for the family.

Marketing With Vision

Let's practice marketing to Hispanics with the great vision that we in the United States have. If a statistic tells us that Hispanics have a higher rate of mobility than the national average, let's show moving companies how to target the market in Spanish. If another statistic informs us that Hispanics live in more crowded quarters and with more family members than the mainstream, let's come up with inexpensive room dividers or cross-over ethnic marketing of futons that fold up and store easily. If we can invent the VCR, the microwave, and the transistor, we can make an optional stovetop with rings so that Mexican customers can make fresh tortillas easily.

Let's continue to move away from the stereotypes that still plague markets in more subtle ways than the Frito Bandito did. And let's advertise to Hispanics with something other than irrelevant, mainstream commercials that are overdubbed.

We need better market research and more accurate data-base information so that we can target our customers and reward their loyalty.

And let's start thinking like Cristina Saralegui, a bilingual talk-show host who is seen on more than six hundred U.S. broadcast and cable stations. Her show is so popular with Hispanic viewers that she's been syndicated in English in twenty-five markets. Cristina thinks that her show can be a vehicle for developing greater tolerance among ethnic groups: "I want my guests to be what they really are, because diversity is what makes this country great."

An Interview With Sonia Green,
Avon Products, Inc.

Here and in Chapters 5 and 6, we will hear top executives of three great American companies tell in their own words how they achieved success for their companies while satisfying the needs of their ethnic customers.

In the first interview, Sonia Maria Green, Director of U.S. Hispanic Marketing for Avon, explains how Avon broke new ground in the Hispanic market.

Q: *Please give a brief history of Avon and indicate its market position.*

SG: Avon is 107 years old. Our history is primarily direct selling, and to this date we are direct selling. Interestingly enough, Avon is the world's largest direct-selling company of cosmetics, fragrances, and toiletries.

Q: *Describe the evolution of your marketing department/programs and bring into that discussion the development of the Hispanic marketing programs.*

SG: Let me take you back to 1988 and 1989, when there was a segmentation department. At that time, I did a couple of cuts or reviews of the population. I looked at black, Hispanic, teen, and mature. We looked at those markets not only from a psychographic but from a demographic perspective.

Also, we correlated all the data with Avon's internal information. I'm very fortunate because all of our representatives are tagged. I know who's Asian, who's black. I know everything about them, which is great. What I don't know is who their ultimate consumer is. When you look at it, what I have are two consumers: the Avon representative, who I service first, and then the ultimate consumer, who benefits from that relationship.

It was our conclusion then that we really needed to focus on the Hispanic market for a lot of reasons. One was the demographics; everyone knows that Hispanics are the fastest-growing group. The fact that Avon owned market share in Latin America—we have a really strong hold there—was another reason. We also had strong brand recognition with the new immigrants coming in from Latin America.

The fact that Hispanics use more cosmetics and toiletries than other types of people has been proven by both internal and external data. All of these things said to us that this is where we would get the best bang for the buck. At that point, we agreed that would be it. As part of the segmentation department we did a little play.

We sell through an Avon brochure. It's not available in Spanish yet. We are the world's second largest distributor of brochures after TV Guide. Up until this point, there was no concrete evidence that we had a demand for a Spanish brochure. Just to give you an idea of what the data bank does for us, I know who is Hispanic and is selecting intentionally English-language materials. And I know who is Hispanic and wants Spanish-language materials. The two of these together give me the whole Hispanic population. That is the degree to which I can quantify everything.

To produce a Spanish brochure meant a major investment. Without a test it was difficult to guarantee to management a certain return on investment.

I played with what we called then an overwrap. We put four pages in the front and four pages in the back overwrapping the brochure and highlighting those items we knew would catch the attention of the Hispanic consumer—items such as cosmetics, fragrances, and toiletries. We know, for example, that classical jewelry doesn't sell. I know that a lot of the items used for decoration in the house doesn't sell.

Another thing our own research revealed is that our Hispanic consumers do not understand the merchandising offers. This is an American phenomenon—buy one, get another one for $5, or get one for equal or lesser value, or for $9.99 with a purchase from pages X to X. So another part of that overwrap was simply to explain what some of these offers were about.

Later, I was able to do a Spanish catalog. Common sense said to me that if I could offer merchandise in Spanish, if I could offer something that I could discount so that representatives would buy them and give them to their best customers, I'd be covered.

As I started working with more people, they were more receptive to the fact that maybe this [Hispanic] segment does react differently. Maybe you don't run The Smartest Shop In Town* campaign and just translate it. But up until then, that is precisely what had happened. Whatever we were doing in the general market, we'd just translate it.

For example, even though the company had selected to go with the general markets advertising agency and to build a major print campaign all around The Smartest Shop In Town, I had a full say in what was appropriate for our market segment. The premise for the campaign, just to give you the idea of what we did, was that one hated going to stores, that one would probably prefer not to deal with salespeople, and that women preferred, when they wanted to buy, to be able to shop anytime they wanted, in a variety of mediums.

But Hispanics like to go shopping. It's a known fact. What do you do on a weekend? You pack up the kids, and you go the nearest mall. The general market campaign did not make sense for Hispanics.

And everyone agreed. The Smartest Shop In Town didn't make any sense. The Hispanic version was ultimately launched as Avon . . . Siempre A Tu Lado (Avon . . . Always By Your Side). We created a TV ad, as well as supporting print program. We took those elements of The Smartest Shop in Town and Hispanicized them, projecting a more contemporary Avon, an Avon that allows you to call by telephone or to buy through the traditional representative visit.

---

*A major campaign that updated Avon's image.

The Hispanic market is right for Avon. We are a high-touch culture. To buy from someone who is your friend or relative or from someone you trust is still very important. In fact, we can see a higher customer service count among Hispanic representatives than others. In the United States, yes, women are not at home, they're tired of salespeople, but that is not true of the Hispanic market. It's still their home, they are reachable, it's still network selling. It's a way of life, it works well. Yet we haven't maximized it.

We had to fix the tagging system. To give you an idea, the district sales manager would sit down with you and if you were like me, Sonia Green, with no accent, she wouldn't even ask you what your culture of origin was. She would just write down white or Anglo, instead of saying, "By the way, Avon has programs sometimes for different market segments to do this properly. Would you please tell me what you consider yourself?" I might have surprised them by saying Hispanic. As a result, we found our numbers of Hispanic customers were underestimates, which was pretty exciting.

It's a traditional problem that everyone faces. Hispanic is a culture. It has nothing to do with race. So we asked in a manner that was identical to the census, identify yourself. Are you black, Asian, Eskimo, whatever it is. And then, are you of Hispanic descent?

We asked more, using question such as "Are you interested in Spanish materials?" We found out that there is an amazing interest among non-Hispanics in Spanish materials.

Q: How did you convince management that Hispanic marketing offered a strong return on investment?

SG: All we had to show them to get their response was a return on investment. We had to show them that for every dollar spent, we could generate some incrementality. You've got to get substantial dollars.

Avon is losing customers nationally, but the Hispanic market is performing better. We're not there yet, but we're much better. You should see this year's results. They're awesome. I love it.

Then we look at it on a regional basis. Avon has five regions: Pasadena, Atlanta, Newark, Morton Grove, and Springdale. Pasadena had an increase in Hispanic sales and a decrease in general market.

Atlanta showed an increase in Hispanic sales and a minimal increase in general market sales. Newark showed an increase versus a decrease. In Morton Grove, Hispanic sales increased, and general sales decreased. There was even an increase in Springdale, *and they said they didn't have any Hispanics,* versus a decrease in general market sales.

With regard to active representatives, I showed an increase in sales to the Hispanic market and a decrease in all others. Average orders consistently showed increases. That was another surprise, and, let's be honest, all that anyone is interested in is the bottom line and what kind of sales you're going to bring in.

Then I did something else. I took another slice at the map, the Avon map. I took the top ten Hispanic divisions. If all I did was concentrate on these top ten—top ten because of their sales to Hispanics—I would be guaranteed more than 50 percent of all Hispanic sales.

I negotiated with the brochure group to increase the representation of Hispanic models. They didn't know what Hispanic models were. I had to give them a presentation and talk to them about finding that generic Hispanic look, which is my challenge.

When we launched our two new products, Agua de Colonia [cologne water] and the "I Love Salsa" audiocassette and compact disc, we knew the offer had to be promoted in our core brochure and netted out on a special insert to make the product pop.

Also, Agua de Colonia from Latin America, which is a favorite fragrance form and does not exist in the U.S. Avon line, was put into the insert with "I Love Salsa."

Q: What do you think a mainstream company needs to do or learn to be successful in ethnic marketing?

SG: Understanding the culture is key. It goes back to something I also believe. I don't think you have to be black to do African-American marketing, and I don't think you have to be Hispanic to do Hispanic marketing. But if you are, you have a competitive advantage. If all things are equal, I would choose the person for who they are and because they understand the nuances. And unless you're very sensitive, you're not going to pick that up.

Q: *Can you elaborate on those elements, such as price, product, and distribution, that may require a different approach when dealing with a cultural segment versus the mainstream market?*

SG: Here's a perfect example, and I think it came up at the product review stage for Agua de Colonia, which, as I mentioned, was launched this year.

Problem No. 1 was, Why do we need another product? Our line is fine. Well, we shared our statistical review of sales of Agua de Colonia for all of Latin America, which showed that there were significant sales, that it is a good fragrance form. The fact that it was in the portfolio for a reason showed it to be a reliable concept. It was part of the core line in Latin America. That made them feel even better.

That was one down. The other problem, was, How do you communicate this? We had a problem. The fragrance house really did not want to pay to put the cologne into the brochure because that meant space and it was a questionable product. We came up with the concept of a Spanish insert. Puerto Rico sells from the U.S. brochure. But when they have new products and offers, they do an insert. So, I said, Why not promote this as they would in Puerto Rico? And we did that.

Speaking about the marketing support, we found out that it wasn't working as well as everyone thought. I put myself in everyone's position. I started calling the 800 number, using the names of everyone in my family, only to discover that not once was that telephone answered by a Hispanic operator or a Spanish-speaking operator, which is more important.

I was able to go back and resolve that problem. We [the Hispanic market] now have our own 800 number, which is always answered by Spanish-speaking operators. These are situations that happen. Usually, even if a promotion is general market, it's fine. We automatically use it, translate it, whatever. But some of us have to say, "Time out." I am not averse to general market things that work. On the contrary. There was one general market campaign that was right for the Hispanic market. And I used it. I merely translated it. It was an ad that we really took to heart and did some fabulous copy for, a full-page spread on lips in all colors of Avon lipstick. Just looking at it, too, with what we know about the Hispanic market, we thought this was right on. And it was wonderful because it was red lips and the copy talks about how Nancy gave her husband a kiss in the morning, then kissed her baby, had breakfast, had lunch, went to several meetings, now look at those lips. It was great. We loved it.

In *Vanidades, Cosmo,* and *Buen Hogar,* we have the inside spread. You open up the magazine and those lips are looking straight at you. The reaction I got from the industry was awesome.

In this particular ad, there was a coupon to turn in to an Avon representative. And you could call if you didn't have an Avon representative. I got a response rate of 11 percent, but is that good or bad? Quite honestly, I encountered a bigger problem. We found out that there wasn't enough Spanish-speaking representatives to give the leads to.

Q: What are the opportunities you see out there for mainstream marketers going into ethnic marketing?

SG: It's just dollars. Avon wouldn't be doing this if it weren't going to positively impact the bottom line, or cash flow. We expect to make money. The P & L [profit and loss] for my activities in my department is going to show some growth and return on investment. Plus, it's a win-win situation for the company and the Hispanic community.

Research shows us that Hispanics have a tendency to buy from those companies that are involved in the community. So there is a psychological thing that is happening. Not only do they want to buy the best products, they want to buy from those companies that are doing things for them. I see every time Avon gets involved in festivals and community events that there is a warm reception from the community.

The Hispanic community needs to leverage its clout. I know I am going to keep winning because they are going to keep coming to me. I just have to keep out there letting them know that I have those breakthrough products. The irony is that they don't know all the things we've talked about, and I've got to let them know that this is what Avon is all about.

Avon has really been a leader in key categories and key product innovations, and nobody knows. The Hispanic woman always wants to make sure that she has the very best product. She is fashionable. Look, the numbers indicate that. They spend so much on makeup and skin-care products. So all I have to do is deliver the message via marketing events and festivals that Avon does have the very best products.

Q: Avon is marketed strictly through direct selling instead of being distributed through retail stores, and it doesn't advertise to the degree that some of your other competitors do. Do you find that this is a limitation of the company?

SG: It's interesting. When you go back to what I said earlier, that the Hispanic culture is still very high-touch and that the 1992 customer service numbers are up, you'll understand that our mode of distribution is still appropriate and in line with the culture. Having people come to you and sit down with you to show you the range of lipstick shades is the same thing you would experience in a retail store. This is just a preference.

Q: **What do you see as the risks for mainstream companies in going into ethnic marketing?**

SG: I think misinformation. There is a lot of stuff that people say, and you don't know who to believe. I'll tell you what happened yesterday, which is a good case in point. I'm doing a joint venture with the Editorial America people, who as you know produce *Vanidades, Buen Hogar,* and *Cosmo* in Spanish—the upgraded magazines. It makes sense for me to get in there if I want to work on my image. I have this arrangement with them so that anyone who subscribes with them for one of their magazines during Christmas gets an Avon premium.

But anyway, I got a call from the account executive, and she said she wanted to talk to me about a problem she was having with someone else. Evidently, there is a major company that has been advertising in *Vista,* advertising in English-speaking Hispanic magazines, and has gotten no results on the ad. This person has been trying to convince the client that maybe it should try to advertise in Spanish.

You can't describe Puerto Ricans as being totally representative of the Hispanic population. I'm Puerto Rican. I'm perfectly bilingual. But Puerto Ricans are not the majority. You saw the chart, the composition. Puerto Ricans are a small segment. The fact of the matter is, most research has shown that the assimilation pattern is not all there. The figure is something like 80 percent or so for partially assimilated or unassimilated Puerto Ricans. Research also shows that Spanish is the preferred language.

One needs to look at the Nielsen and SRC [Strategy Research Corp.] ratings to see what's going on with Spanish-language television shows. But Linda Chavez comes along and she gets quoted as a research expert and there is no counterbalance.

Marketing strategy research has also proven the existence of something called re-acculturation. This is me. Spanish, believe it or not, is the language spoken in *my* house. I want to make sure that my kids have that com-

petitive advantage. I know that in the long run they are
going to be far more valuable because of that second
language. And we are doing it intentionally. And let me
tell you, I am not the only one. I can point to zillions of
people who are back into this. We are going back to Latin
America for our travel. We prefer it. I want to go where I
can speak my language and enjoy myself.

There is also a phenomenon that is occurring that
people cannot quantify precisely. Yes, I watch "Golden
Girls" and "Cheers"—those are my favorite shows. But I
also watch Spanish shows—my husband prefers the Spanish news. My husband, an Argentine, watches the soccer
games from Latin America on the weekends.

That is the problem I think the general market has—
who to believe, because we don't have people like me who
are involved in marketing to Hispanics.

5

Marketing to Asian-Americans

Imagine a car ad targeting the Japanese expatriate community in Scarsdale, New York, explaining how buying a certain luxury model will make a person stand out from the crowd. Or consider an ad aimed at Chinese-American small businesses in Monterey Park, California, that trumpets the advantages of new, improved telecommunications technology over outdated computer systems. Finally, imagine an ad by a retailer of sound systems that's targeted at New York City's sizable Korean population and that boasts about "the best Japanese state-of-the-art audio technology."

Sound good? The businesses that advertised these goods and services certainly might think so. In fact, I made these ads up, although they are all based on ads targeted to the general market. Not only are they fictitious, they would be disastrous if ever actually used.

What's wrong with them? The first ad says that buying a particular car will make you "stand out from the crowd." But in Japan, people believe that they should keep a low profile and not attempt to call attention to themselves for heroism or achievement. In Confucian societies, the group is the unit of importance, not the individual.

The second pitch, touting technology that is "new, improved, and better than the competition," is not necessarily desirable in communities where being old and reliable is often preferable to being new and without a track record. And knocking the competition hurts everyone, setting up a win-lose rather than a win-win situation.

Finally, as a result of the Japanese occupation of Korea during World War II, Koreans have a long-standing resentment toward things Japanese. Ads directed to Koreans should not boast of the Japanese origin of their products.

The Fastest-Growing Market

Marketers can't afford mistakes like these, because the Asian-American community is the fastest-growing market in the United States when measured in percentages. The Asian-American community grew by nearly 110 percent from 1980 to 1990. During the same period, the Hispanic population increased 53 percent, the African-American population, 13 percent, and the non-Hispanic white population, just 4 percent.

The official Asian-American count in the 1990 census was 7.3 million people, but, as with Hispanics, this is considered a vast undercount. Unofficial estimates of the Asian-American population were close to 10 million by 1992. The Urban Institute of Washington, D.C., estimates that by 2010 there will be more than 17 million Asian-Americans in the U.S.

Asians will continue to immigrate in large numbers as a result of the Refugee Act of 1980. Larger numbers of Vietnamese, Cambodians, and Laotians will arrive in coming years. While the percentages of Chinese, Japanese, Koreans, Asian Indians, and Filipino immigrants in the population are expected to remain constant or even to decline slightly by 2000, the percentages of Vietnamese and "other" Asians are expected to increase.

Affluence and Education

Some Asian immigrants are highly affluent and quite well-educated. Although many Vietnamese, Cambodians, and Laotians are below the median U.S. income level, immigrants from Taiwan and Hong Kong rank above it. The overall poverty rate for Asian-American families was only 11 percent in 1991, compared with close to 30 percent for black families, 26.5 percent for Hispanic families, and 8.8 percent for white families.

The majority of Asian-Americans are quite affluent and have a median household income approaching $40,000. More than 35 percent of Asian households have incomes of $50,000 or more, compared with about 25 percent of white households. However, individual (as distinguished from household) incomes are lower than those of whites. Keep in mind that the median household income of whites in the same period was about $32,000.

One reason for the higher household income of Asian-Americans is that more Asian-Americans have more people in the household and in the workforce. Close to 78 percent of all Asian-Americans live in married-couple households in which at least two people work. The overall divorce rate is low, and the majority of Asian-Americans marry other Asians. Great respect is afforded older people, and it's not unusual to have three generations living under one roof.

Asian-Americans have a very high college-completion rate of 39 percent, compared to about 17 percent for the general population, according to the Census Bureau. With high household income and advanced levels of education, most Asian-Americans don't look for off-brand bargains when shopping. They are often loyal to brand names, which many believe stand for quality and prestige.

Asian-Americans are good customers for educational offerings, real estate, financial services, electronics, and other high-priced items. Real estate is a popular investment for many Asians because "it's something tangible, and it's something that represents wealth," according to Eleanor Yu, president and CEO of AdLand and AdLand Worldwide of San Francisco.

Many Vietnamese buy a good deal of jewelry because, having experienced war and political turmoil in their country, they believe that they should invest in something they can convert back to cash if they need money quickly. State-of-the-art technology is also popular, more so than for the mainstream market, probably because of Asian-Americans' high levels of education and income. Asian-Americans are great consumers

of audio components, video equipment, computers, sophisticated appliances, and telecommunications equipment.

Targeted Marketing Campaigns

Smart marketers such as Equitable, Metropolitan Life, and New
York Life Insurance advertise in Asian-language media and
have bilingual Asian sales agents. (See the interview with Met
Life's Bill Orton at the end of this chapter.) New York Life runs
"lifestyle" ads featuring Asian-Americans; Bank of America in
Los Angeles offers product literature in at least three Asian
languages as part of its effort to capture some of the Asian-
Americans' savings.

Asian-Americans aren't just a good market for expensive
goods and services. They are often brand-loyal consumers of
inexpensive commodity-type products as well. Savvy marketers such as Colgate-Palmolive, whose toothpastes are sold in
Asia, capitalize on brand loyalty and target Asian immigrants
to the U.S.

Anheuser-Busch, world-famous for beer, also sells rice
through its agricultural division. It has developed eight varie-
ties of California rice, which it targets at eight Asian nationalities. Anheuser-Busch's ads zero in on the differences among
the Asian groups and contain culturally appropriate copy for
each group.

For the most part, however, Asian-Americans have been
ignored by most mainstream marketers, who are unaware of
their buying power, fearful of spending money to reach a small
market segment, or convinced that Asian-Americans' education and income automatically make them part of the general
market.

Some marketers say that Asian-Americans will see and
respond to ads in mainstream publications and television.
Others say that there aren't enough data to plan a marketing
campaign targeted to Asians. And many point to the diversity
among the Asian-American population, which includes Chinese, Filipinos, Japanese, Koreans, Vietnamese, Asian-Indians,

and others, and argue that the market is too subsegmented to justify investing advertising dollars.

This is a big mistake. There's a good deal of evidence that even assimilated Asians prefer to see ads featuring people with whom they can identify. Although we are beginning to see a fair amount of African-Americans in mainstream advertising, few, if any, ads feature Asian-Americans. One of the few advertisers to appeal to Asian-Americans is San Francisco's Bank of America. BofA covers all its bases by running ads for its services in Chinese-language print media and on TV and also running home-equity loan ads featuring Asian-Americans in English-language newspapers.

Joseph Lam, president of L3 advertising in New York and Los Angeles, has found that most of the Asian market does not read English-language newspapers and is not comfortable with obtaining information only from English-language sources. Many Asian-Americans, if not assimilated completely, have at least acculturated and integrated into the mainstream population. Nevertheless, they may still prefer in-language ads.

Penetrating Insular Communities

Some Asian-American communities exhibit an insularity that is hard to penetrate, seeing other Americans of any ethnic or racial background as cultural outsiders. Many people who have lived in New York's self-sufficient Chinatown all their lives have had only rare encounters with people outside the Chinese community.

But even this insularity can be a bonanza for marketers who take the time to target their ads properly. Many Asian-Americans rely heavily on word of mouth and on the recommendations of their peer group.

Dr. Diane Simpson, president of Simpson International of New York and an expert on the Asian market, explains that peer group influence is one example of collective behavior: "Research has shown that in an apartment building, it's not unusual for all the Korean-American occupants to use the same detergent."

Choi Lee and Robert T. Green, commenting in the *International Journal of International Business Studies* about the difference between marketing to group-centered Asian cultures and marketing to the U.S. mainstream with its individualistic culture said, "Group acceptance of a product will often be an essential forerunner of acceptance in the marketplace."

Segmenting the Market Is a Must

Although there are underlying similarities among Asian cultures, marketers must subsegment the Asian-American community. In the past, some advertisers used "Suzy Wong" ads, showing a beautiful woman in a slit dress (cheong-sam) snuggled up to a dragon to depict an Asian woman. Today, savvy marketers often must come up with at least seven different ads to cover the six major groups: Filipino, Japanese, Korean, Vietnamese, Asian Indian, and Chinese (who need two separate campaigns because they may speak Mandarin or Cantonese).

This kind of subsegmenting requires a little knowledge of history and culture, but nothing that requires years of research. It's pretty hard for advertisers to justify ignorance such as that shown in a campaign for footwear a few years ago, which depicted Japanese women performing the ancient practice of footbinding. Not only did this ad stereotype Japanese people as "Shogun" characters, it displayed the company's ignorance about Asian cultures; footbinding was practiced exclusively in China.

The Six Asian Markets

Find/SVP, a data vendor in New York, breaks the Asian market into six markets: (1) Filipinos, the largest and arguably the best assimilated Asian-American group; (2) Chinese, who tend to divide into two groups, identified by the Chinese themselves as American Born Chinese (ABC), who are well-to-do and quite assimilated, and Fresh Off Boats (FOB), who are blue-collar, conservative, and patriarchal; (3) Japanese, including both those who have lived in the United States (especially California) for generations and foreign-born Japanese, often on assignment, most of whom live in the New York region; (4) Koreans, who tend to cluster in large metropolitan areas and are often small-business owners; (5) Vietnamese, who are the fastest growing Asian group and one-third of whom live in California; (6) Asian Indians, often highly educated professionals, who are not as geographically clustered as the other Asian groups.

The diversity doesn't stop there. A total of twenty-nine distinct Asian groups make up the Asian-American market. No one is suggesting that a separate marketing campaign should be designed to reach each of these subgroups. "The important thing is for marketers to realize that there is no such thing as the Asian-American market inasmuch as there is no common language or culture," says Doug Alligood, vice president at BBDO, an ad agency in New York, speaking in *Marketing News.*

Levels of Assimilation Among Asians

Clearly, the complex Asian market is highly segmented, especially when generational and assimilation/acculturation issues are taken into consideration. Second-generation Chinese-Americans, concentrated in the suburbs, frequently speak English, and may not even speak Chinese at home.

Chinese and other Asian-Americans living in integrated neighborhoods are relatively assimilated by the second and certainly by the third generation. Second- and third-generation Chinese-Americans often grow up drinking milk, even though some first-generation Asians are lactose-intolerant. My friend Jane Lee often suggests we meet for a frozen yogurt lunch in the summer.

Contrast that with Chinese-Americans who are concentrated in America's Chinatowns and who may speak primarily Chinese throughout the generations, eat only traditional Chinese food, buy goods imported from China, and use only services from Chinese-Americans vendors and providers.

Almost 90 percent of Korean-Americans are foreign-born, the majority having immigrated after 1965. Korean immigrants are still coming to the United States in great numbers, moving in with families and keeping the language alive.

Second- and third-generation Japanese-Americans (*nisei* and *sansei*) are highly assimilated and make up a very different market from the transient Japanese "salarymen" who live in the United States for a few years and then return to Japan. The salarymen's children, however, go to school in the United States and become acculturated, at least on the surface, to American ways. There is also an intermediate market of Japanese professionals and students who are fairly long-term residents but who are less highly assimilated than the *nisei* and *sansei*.

Different Languages, Religions, Races

The primary Asian groups and their subgroups do not all share similar languages, religions, or even race. Asian Indians, although their homeland is part of Asia geographically, are not Asian racially but are considered Caucasian. Furthermore, their religions are not rooted in Confucianism; they are usually Hindu, Moslem, Buddhist, or Jain. To complicate things further, within the Asian Indian subgroups there are at least thirty known languages. (Since there are close to 1 billion people in India, this should not be surprising.)

An Indian client of mine brought some clerical workers from India to staff an office in White Plains, New York. All of the senior managers spoke Hindi and English (the most widely used of India's sixteen official languages), as well as one or more regional languages. I noted, however, that the clerical workers never spoke Indian languages among themselves. One of the managers explained that they communicated with each other only in English because, although each spoke several Indian languages, they had no language in common except English.

Chinese also speak a number of dialects that are not mutually understood. Chinese from Hong Kong speak Cantonese, while the Taiwanese speak Mandarin. Filipinos speak English and one of at least three other distinct languages. Curiously, spoken Korean is one of the few Asian languages not related linguistically to those used in other East Asian countries.

Historical Conflicts

Marketers must take care not to lump Asian-American groups together or to confuse one group with another. Many Asian-Americans harbor centuries-long hostilities toward other Asian nationalities, the result of wars and occupations. To make things more difficult, along with animosities among Asian groups, there is hostility within groups.

Hanh Hoang, writing in *Transpacific* magazine, says, "Contrary to the non-Asians' image of a homogeneous Asian group, Asian-Americans are quite diverse in their background, lifestyle, and thinking. They often live in different communities that have little contact with each other. Differences in national origin, generations, politics, degree of acculturation, or gender still fuel prejudices started years ago in places far from the U.S."

Using Media Effectively

Unfortunately, when companies do attempt to target Asian-American segments, they make all the usual flubs and mistakes made when marketers try to save money by having cultural interpretations and language translations done by amateurs. One company placed an ad in Chinese newspapers to wish the community a happy New Year; the printers dropped the line of type and replaced it incorrectly so that they wound up wishing readers a "Year New Happy." Another advertiser used Korean models when advertising to the Vietnamese community in Los Angeles. Koreans, who have different lineage, rarely look anything like the Vietnamese. Another U.S. company that manufactures sporting equipment packaged golf balls for export to Japan in a special four-pack promotional deal, instead of in the usual three-pack. They didn't know that four is considered bad luck because the sound of the word for four (in both Japanese and Chinese) is close to the sound of the word for death.

Clearly this very desirable but highly segmented market can't be reached effectively through mass-market channels. Although many Asian-Americans are reached through mainstream media, many others are not. There are literally thousands of target-language radio, television, and print media to advertise in, and they are relatively inexpensive.

Joe Lam of L3 says, "Newspapers are very powerful in Asian communities. For Asian and especially Chinese consumers, print media is strongest on the East Coast because it is more established than radio or TV. But San Francisco and Los Angeles support more established radio and television networks, along with newspapers."

A little known but effective and low-cost method of reaching Asian-Americans is by sideband radio. In some big cities, advertisers lease unused portions of other stations' FM channels to run programming in Asian languages. Listeners use special radio receivers, usually sold by neighborhood businesses. There's a multiplier effect for a company that reaches out through both in-language and mainstream media, since many Asian-Americans read publications and watch television in both English and their native language.

Common Denominators

For marketers who have subsegmented the increasingly overtapped mainstream into micromarkets, it won't be difficult to extend that process to Asian-American segments and to capitalize on the opportunity to increase sales. Total Asian-American household income is higher than the U.S. average, which means greater purchasing power. Furthermore, if you capture a segment and customers become loyal to your brand, that loyalty will be spread by word of mouth to others, especially new immigrants who move in with or near to your customer base.

Where do we start when we decide to go after this market? By looking for some common denominators, ways to make the job a little easier. Asia is huge, with billions of people, but, for historical reasons, its peoples have many cultural similarities, which simplifies our task. One of these is the family or group focus. In collectivist or "we" cultures, the family or group culture is far more important than the individual, while the individual dominates "I" cultures like the U.S.

Confucianism

One unifying factor is Confucianism (although most Filipinos are Roman Catholic and most Asian Indians are Hindu or Moslem). Confucianism, however, is the major religious influence on Chinese, Japanese, Korean, and Vietnamese cultures. In addition to its group focus, Confucianism emphasizes respect for authority, especially for parents and teachers; hard work; discipline and the ability to delay gratification; harmony in all things; and long-term reciprocal relationships.

Asian-Americans have higher rates of business ownership than the overall U.S. population. There are almost ninety Korean-owned businesses for every one thousand Koreans in the United States, compared to about sixty-five businesses per one thousand people in the general population. Seventy of every one thousand Asian Indians own businesses, and Japanese and Chinese own businesses at a rate slightly higher than the national average.

Relationship Selling

In marketing and selling to Asian business owners, the relationship counts for everything. And while Asians very much like to do business with other Asians, anyone who makes an effort to appeal to their needs will be warmly welcomed. Cold calling and reaching out without some form of connection to the individual or group, on the other hand, won't work.

A company or salesperson, must, in some way, get involved with the particular segment it wants to reach. Advertising in Asian media, having a good record in hiring Asians and in serving the Asian community, or, ideally, having an influential contact are all good ways to begin penetrating this complex market. Once a connection is made, it's important to remember that for most Asian-Americans, the things that count are quality, a good and long-standing reputation, and respect for the customer.

An important selling point for most Asian-Americans is the reputation of the company. Long-standing, established companies with a history of service are usually preferred over start-up operations, since age and experience are highly valued by most Asians. And if a business is family-owned, then so much the better; both tradition and respect for family count for a great deal. Once a product or service is adopted by one satisfied purchaser, it is easy to win acceptance by a larger segment of the market.

This doesn't mean that a new company can't capture Asian-American business. But it needs to cultivate a relationship of mutual respect slowly and patiently, perhaps even more than a long-established company does, before making a sales pitch.

As with the Hispanic market, an excellent way to reach Asian-Americans is through sponsorship, scholarships, contributions to benevolent societies, special promotions, and participation in religious holiday celebrations and community events.

The majority of Asians prefer factual messages in advertising and personal selling over emotional pitches. Asian-Americans consider it poor form to display emotions in public. Lack of understanding of these cultural values, coupled with the mainstream assumptions that if Asians don't express emotion, they must not be feeling any, has given rise to the stereotype of the "stony-faced, inscrutable Asian."

Successful Marketing Campaigns

Segmenting and targeting the Asian market should begin with the design of the product or service. For example, Asian women, especially recent immigrants, are generally smaller than mainstream American women. In Los Angeles and San Francisco, many stores stock large quantities of high-quality petite-size clothing. In the San Francisco Bay area, 36 percent of Asian-Americans named Macy's as their favorite store. Macy's went out of its way to serve Asian women, according to Eleanor Yu of Adland, and has been rewarded by loyal customers. Ms. Yu goes on to say, "Once you win brand loyalty of the Asian-American, you have a customer for life."

Targeting Korean-Americans, Peterson Bank in Chicago has formed a department dedicated to the needs of its Korean customers. All the department's employees speak Korean, and promotional materials are available in both Korean and English. Peterson Bank was the first in the country to install a bilingual telephone banking service. It buys spots on a local cable television station that runs blocks of Korean programming. Korean customers are avid consumers of mortgages, business loans, home equity lines of credit, and savings plans. The bank has what it calls a Rose Account, which works like a Christmas Club and resembles similar programs found in Korea.

Remy Martin, like Colgate and other global companies, has capitalized on its name recognition among certain immigrants. Cognac is popular in Hong Kong, for example, because the Chinese have traditionally associated the grape with hot foods, which are considered fiery, masculine, and potent. However because Chinese prefer strong liquor, they prefer cognac to wine.

In this country, Remy Martin's Chinese-language ads portray its brand as a prestige drink. The New York ad agency L3 arranges for Remy to sponsor the Moon Festival banquet, a very important celebration in Chinese culture. These banquets are attended by leaders who are influential in the community. The Moon Festival ads feature fruits and cakes, which are traditional elements of the Chinese holiday, against the background of the Brooklyn Bridge. Located near New York's Chinatown, the bridge symbolizes the "bridging" of traditions, East and West. As a result of these efforts, Remy Martin XO Cognac, despite its price of $110 a bottle, flies off the shelves in Chinatown.

Paul Sladkus, who operates a New York ad agency, recently received some corporate grants to research Asian-American markets. Not surprisingly, he found that even though participants in the research had a median income close to $50,000, were white-collar professionals, and used English most frequently in the workplace, their native language continued to play an important role in their culture and home life.

Some marketing specialists believe companies should have programs to appeal even to third- and fourth-generation Asians, but they find strong resistance from advertisers. Joe Lam, whose agency created the Remy Martin cognac ad, said in *The Wall Street Journal*, "Even those Asians born in the United States, who are highly assimilated, prefer to see people in ads that they can identify with."

From Chinatown to Suburbia

Some of the difficulty of segmenting the Asian market is offset by the ease of locating the target market. Many Asian-Americans are geographically concentrated. While there are Asians in every state, nine states (California, Hawaii, New York, Illinois, New Jersey, Texas, Florida, Michigan, and Washington) have the largest Asian-American populations. And the cluster narrows: 55 percent of all Asian-Americans live in California, the greater New York area, or Honolulu.

Even in these areas, Asian-Americans do not live only in the insular enclaves of Chinatowns or Little Tokyos. Asian-Americans live in integrated, mainstream neighborhoods, as well as in neighborhoods heavily populated by assimilated and acculturated Asians. Japanese-Americans have moved into some of the wealthiest neighborhoods of Los Angeles. Chinese-Americans live not only in Chinatown but also in New York's and New Jersey's priciest suburbs.

And although most Asians are still clustered in certain areas, some are moving into places where few Asians have lived. Minneapolis, New Orleans, California's Central Valley, and other secondary markets are attracting significant communities of Asian-Americans, opening up new opportunities for marketers who use geodemographic databases.

Chinese-Americans

As with all immigrant populations, it's difficult to get an exact count of the number of Asians in the United States. The official count of Chinese-Americans is somewhere around 1.6 million, but unofficial estimates go up to about 2 million. Chinese account for close to 20 percent of the Asian-Americans in the United States. About one third live in the traditional China-towns of New York, San Francisco, and other cities.

The Chinese first came to the United States during the California Gold Rush of the 1850s, and later they helped build the transcontinental railroad. The majority of these early immigrants came from what is now called Guangdong, the region then known as Canton.

By 1880 a little over a quarter of a million Chinese had been admitted to the United States. Chinese were the first immigrant group to be legally barred from the United States (by the Chinese Exclusion Act of 1892). In 1965 the immigration laws, which still barred almost all Asian immigrants while admitting Europeans, were changed. The new law imposes a quota for Asian immigration that exceeds the quota for immigrants from Central and South America.

Since 1965 large numbers of Chinese immigrants from Hong Kong and Taiwan, as well as from mainland China, have arrived in the United States, along with ethnic Chinese from Malaysia, Singapore, Indonesia, Burma, Thailand, Vietnam, Cambodia, the Philippines, and even Latin America, creating an ethnic stew not even dreamed of in the early years of the twentieth century.

The Chinese are a fairly segmented market of languages and religions. Many of the new immigrants speak different dialects and can't understand one another. The early immigrants, who usually speak Cantonese, often complain that they are beginning to feel like strangers as Chinatowns fill up with new immigrants who speak Mandarin or other dialects.

ABCs and FOBs

The most important divisions among Chinese immigrants are class, education, and locale. I prefer to call the two main subsegments Suburban Chinese and Downtown Chinese, although the Chinese themselves often use the terms American Born Chinese (ABC) and Fresh Off the Boat (FOB).

Most Downtown Chinese are recent immigrants, but some were born in this country. They live in Chinatowns or in small insular communities. Suburban Chinese are most often born in America and live in relatively integrated and often upscale communities. However, some relatively new immigrants from Taiwan and Hong Kong may be fresh off the boat, but are nonetheless upscale and suburban.

Suburban Chinese-Americans enjoy the highest earnings of all Asian-Americans, thanks to their white-collar, professional, technical, and sales positions. Downtown Chinese who are often, but not always, foreign born, tend to have lower hourly earnings and are usually employed in services and in manufacturing as retail, restaurant, and factory workers. New immigrants frequently come to the Chinatowns but often leave once they learn English and save enough money.

Legal and undocumented newcomers to Chinatowns in Chicago, New York, and San Francisco keep expanding these "downtowns." And some American-born Chinese do stay in the Chinatowns, adding to the stability and growth of these neighborhoods.

In New York's Chinatown, the residents are mostly first-generation; 80 percent are foreign-born. But on the weekends, suburban Chinese from the outer boroughs of New York City and from the suburbs of New Jersey and Connecticut come to Chinatown to celebrate birthdays and holidays. Other great centers of Chinese-Americans include San Francisco; Monterey Park, a suburb of Los Angeles, with a population that is more than 60 percent Chinese-American; Flushing, a neighborhood in the New York City borough of Queens; Napierville, in Chicago; and Sharpstown, in Houston.

Cultural Issues

Many assimilated suburban Chinese-Americans are frustrated when they are mistaken for new immigrants or for other, non-

Chinese Asians. What an opportunity for the marketer who takes the time needed to subsegment this group and properly target products, advertising, and promotional campaigns!

Even with the differences among the Chinese-American subsegments, there are strong cultural similarities that can be used as a basis for marketing outreach. The family is the center of the social structure. Even among second- and third-generation Chinese-Americans, there is great emphasis on familial relationships and obligations. Whether upscale suburban or downscale downtown, Chinese-Americans save and invest for their children's education and the care of relatives, which is considered an obligation.

Many parents still expect children to live with them until they marry. Grown men and women are sometimes expected to live with and/or take care of aging parents. Chinese-Americans often send money to relatives still living in Asia. Just before the Chinese New Year, people line up at banks to withdraw money for relatives thousands of miles away.

Like many other ethnic and minority groups, for many years Chinese-Americans were discouraged from depositing money in U.S. banks; only white people's money was green enough for mainstream bankers. The Chinese in turn developed credit associations that acted as a kind of informal bank. It's because of these "banks" that many Chinese were able to become entrepreneurs.

Today there is still a reluctance on the part of the more insular Chinese-Americans to use banks that are outside the community. Some still prefer to put cash into safe deposit boxes than into bank accounts. Financial institutions that go out of their way to woo this still insular segment can enjoy a windfall.

Just as mainstream America has lucky and unlucky numbers, so too many Chinese believe in lucky numbers and colors. For the Chinese, green symbolizes growth, and gold means prosperity. Red is also considered a good color by the Chinese; during the New Year celebrations, children are given red envelopes containing money. If your research points to a targeted direct-mail campaign, it's a good idea to send direct-mail pitches in other than white envelopes, because white usually symbolizes death.

For Chinese from Hong Kong, blue and white usually mean a celebration. Also, Chinese consider the number 8 to be good luck. (The Cantonese word for 8 rhymes with the word for prosperity.) Because of this affection for lucky numbers, it's worthwhile to evaluate the use of sweepstakes, lotteries, and contests in a marketing program aimed at Chinese-Americans.

The "Eight Bigs"

Chinese-Americans get what they want in the good old American way—by saving and investing wisely. In New York's Chinatown, people want and get what they call the "eight bigs"— a color television, a refrigerator, a car, a VCR, a camera, a set of furniture, a telephone, and a washing machine.

Knowing this can translate into a gold mine for marketers of durable goods who want to target this segment. One survey of Chinese-Americans' consumer buying behavior found that, in most instances, both husband and wife made the decision to buy. (About 85 percent of Chinese-Americans are married, and fewer than 10 percent are divorced.) Rarely was the purchasing decision made by one partner alone. Recommendations of friends were very important sources of information, along with advertising and *Consumer Report*-type magazines.

Mike Quon, a successful third-generation Chinese-American New York graphic designer, says, "We're in the background, but we're a growing part of the American future." His ethnicity has sometimes attracted clients who associate the Chinese culture with superior quality and persistence. "We certainly know quality, price, and value, so sell to us, acknowledge us; we're out here," Quon says.

Advertising to the Chinese

Although many Chinese-Americans read and speak English, they don't always identify with the content of English-language ads. With the exception of the successful Reebok ad featuring the Chinese-American tennis great Michael Chang, few if any ads target or depict Asian-Americans. (A short time after that ad came out, Reebok's sales to Asian-Americans skyrocketed.)

Like most ethnic market segments, Chinese-Americans who can't identify with ads and who feel the ads are not for them have little incentive to buy that particular brand. In addition to mainstream print, many Chinese-Americans regularly read Chinese-language newspapers and periodicals, making these good ways to reach this highly desirable subsegment.

Filipinos

Unlike Chinese and other Asian-Americans, Filipinos do not have a clear image in the minds of mainstream Americans. With a 1990 population of close to 2 million, or about 21 percent of the Asian-Americans in the United States, there are almost as many Filipinos in the United States as Chinese-Americans, yet they are a good deal less visible. One reason for Filipinos' lack of a clear image is Philippine history, which is a story of conquest and colonization. Some Filipinos have assimilated into the culture of their Spanish grandparents, some into the culture of their Japanese parents, and some into the culture of their former American colonizers. Some have adopted a mixture of these and other cultures. Filipinos are ethnically Malay, and the Philippines are geographically part of South Asia. But as a result of more than four hundred years of Spanish domination, most Filipinos are Catholic and have Spanish surnames. (During these centuries, Chinese, Indonesians, Arabs, and others also settled on the islands.) The Philippines were colonized by the United States for almost forty-five years and then were occupied by the Japanese during World War II, further adding to the ethnic mix. As a result, the ethnic background of many Filipinos—like that of many Americans—is a mixture of two or more traditions.

Filipino Invisibility

Filipinos, particularly those on the West Coast, say they are often confused with Mexican-Americans because of their Spanish surnames. One participant in a seminar I gave recently in Los Angeles complained that she was constantly getting direct mail in Spanish and being pitched to on the phone in Spanish because her last name is Garcia. Ms. Garcia, who was born in California, is a native speaker of English and understands some Tagalog, one of the principal languages of the Philippines, but she doesn't speak Spanish. She cites this confusion as a marker of Filipino invisibility.

One of the biggest problems for any marketer who mistakenly thinks that Ms. Garcia is Hispanic is that she will remember the company's name and probably never buy its products or services. Many Filipinos hope that they will become more visible thanks to recent well-educated immigrants and American-born Filipinos, who they hope will band together to make their identity more prominent.

Harry H. S. Kitano, co-author of *Asian Americans: Emerging Minorities*, believes that Filipinos' invisibility is the result of factors other than economics and heritage: "Many Filipinos already speak English so that in a way they don't need an ethnic community as much as other groups."

History

Philippine history is a catalog of occupation and colonization. The goal of the four-hundred-year colonization by Spain was to spread Christianity, and in fact close to 85 percent of the population is Roman Catholic. The Philippines is the only Christian nation in Asia.

All those years of Spanish domination had a strong effect on cultural values. The Spanish version of Roman Catholicism, with its fatalistic bent, has left its mark on the Philippine people. Filipinos share several cultural traditions with Hispanics, including courtship rituals, holidays such as Christmas and other Christian festivals, and the emphasis on family.

Immigration

The Philippines became independent in 1946. Ongoing political instability has led many educated and professional Filipinos to immigrate to the United States since then. This upscale group stands in contrast to the Filipino immigrants who came to the United States before World War II, most of whom were students or unskilled laborers.

The oldest and largest Filipino communities are in San Francisco and Los Angeles, and there is a large Filipino community in Chicago that was established in 1920 by railroad workers. The West Coast is still a popular destination for newly arrived unskilled and semiskilled Filipino immigrants. The East Coast Filipino community is concentrated in New York, New Jersey, and Connecticut, and a number of Filipino families have settled in the area between Baltimore, Maryland, and Norfolk, Virginia.

Many of the early Filipino immigrants were awarded citizenship right after World War II and were able to go to college and to move up the economic ladder. By 1970 other highly educated young Filipinos, many of whom had attended professional schools in the United States, began immigrating in search of economic opportunity, creating a "brain drain." Many settled in California, Hawaii, and Chicago and along the East Coast.

The East Coast Filipino community, which numbers around 250,000, is a highly educated, professional group that includes many doctors, nurses, engineers, teachers, and accountants. Interestingly, Filipino women have the highest rates of college completion and of employment of all Asian-American women.

Cultural Issues

Filipinos represent the best of the Hispanic and Asian cultures and have much in common with Hispanics. Most are very outgoing and sociable people. They love to have a good time and appreciate a good laugh. When advertising and promoting to Filipinos, it's a good idea to incorporate humor to appeal to this segment.

A successful marketing campaign targeted at Filipinos uses a family structure, humor, and a classy approach. Most important, it reaches out to the local community and social organizations and shows recognition of Filipinos' distinctiveness. The campaign can be done in English, and the costs are low for the return—a loyal customer.

Korean-Americans

Before Koreans came to New York and opened lush greengroceries, I had to travel across town to get fruits or vegetables in the winter (except for some shriveled potatoes and wilted iceberg lettuce). Now, thanks to the entrepreneurial spirit of the Korean-American community, I can encourage my husband to eat fresh vegetables and fruit with me all year long, even though he would probably rather be eating a "well-balanced" meal of a cheeseburger, french fries, and a pickle.

Korean-Americans do much more, however, than satisfy my cravings for mangos and papayas in December. As an article in *Crain's New York Business* reports, the New York Korean-American community includes owners of thousands of businesses such as dry cleaners, nail salons, fish markets, and garment manufacturers. The Korean-American Small Business Center of New York represents ten thousand Korean-Americans in twenty-three different industries.

History

There are over 1 million Korean-Americans in the United States, of whom close to 90 percent are foreign-born. Koreans account for about 13 percent of the Asian-Americans in the United States. In the late nineteenth and early twentieth centuries, Koreans came to the United States seeking political asylum and to work the Hawaiian sugar plantations. A small number immigrated between 1910 and 1918, fleeing Japanese oppression. For the next thirty years or so, while most Asians were restricted from entering the United States, Korea was occupied by Japan and later suffered the division of the country into North and South and the Korean War. By the 1950s, larger numbers of Koreans had begun immigrating to the United States.

Between 1965 and 1970, close to twenty-five thousand Koreans came to the United States. Most were highly educated professionals between twenty and forty-four years of age who settled in California.

About thirty thousand South Korean immigrants come to the United States each year, and New York, Los Angeles, Honolulu, Chicago, and other major cities have growing populations of Koreans and Korean-Americans.

The Korean Work Ethic

Korea is a Confucian society, with a strong work ethic. Some of the Korean-owned fruit markets in New York stay open twenty-four hours day, staffed by members of one family. Korean-Americans work very hard, averaging around a fifty-five-hour workweek, but in New York the average Korean greengrocer works eleven hours a day, six days a week! Koreans have the highest self-employment rate of any Asian immigrant group. In fact, according to the Census Bureau, they have the highest business-ownership rate of any ethnic or racial group, including whites.

But this hard work and high rate of self-employment make for a quite insular, not to mention tired, target group. Occupational stress often plagues Korean-Americans and can affect their family relationships, which are extremely important to them. Marketers should reach out to Korean-Americans by referring to their need for time-saving devices.

Maybe because they are so driven, Korean-Americans sometimes appear more brusque and direct than do Chinese-Americans. They are also somewhat more individualistic than most Asian-Americans. Korean-Americans are tough bargainers and more willing to give a direct "no" than other Asian-Americans. However, they, too, prefer the soft sell in ads as well as in making face-to-face purchases.

In addition to its strong work ethic, the Korean culture emphasizes self-reliance and family loyalty; families may provide financial support, employees, and, sometimes, unpaid laborers. Koreans also value education highly, respect their elders, and praise frugality.

When they want to borrow money to open businesses, some Koreans use the kye, a system of revolving credit that can be traced back to sixteenth-century Korean farming villages. Like the Chinese, many Koreans prefer kye over banks and government aid because of their ethnic pride and their suspicion of banks (based on bad experiences with banking practices in Korea and fear of U.S. Internal Revenue audits of their often cash-based businesses).

Korean Assimilation

Most Koreans who arrive in the United States today are highly educated, but many speak little or no English. They feel strongly about keeping their cultural traditions and values intact. In fact, some Koreans, like some other immigrant groups, are resistant to the idea of assimilation to the American culture.

The reasons for this may be varied. One possibility is that a number of Koreans see their stay in the United States as temporary. Dr. Diane Simpson says, "When people look at immigration rates, they don't usually look at emigration from the U.S. They simply assume that immigrants are here to stay. That may not be the case with all groups. Marketers should research what the group's intention is for staying in the U.S. Even if people think they might go back to their homeland, they can change their minds. In the case of some Korean immigrants, it's important to know how they view themselves—as Koreans or Korean-Americans. Some Koreans may see that economic opportunity is growing in Korea and decide to return there."

Since many Koreans are first-generation, the language barrier and the absence of a long-standing community identity in the United States may slow the acculturation process. For the most part, Korean-Americans read Korean language newspapers, watch Korean programming on TV, eat at Korean-owned restaurants, and shop at Korean-owned stores. Often the first-generation mother in a Korean family doesn't learn to speak English, slowing the acculturation process even more.

Koreans have little exposure to national brands because most mainstream advertisers haven't targeted this still mostly first- and second-generation segment. Marketers may find that ads in Korean media are especially cost-effective. Although many second-generation Korean-Americans speak English, a large percentage of the Korean-American population sub-scribes to in-language media. Reaching out to the merchant associations and to Chambers of Commerce, where community influencers are found, is an especially effective way to gain entry to this valuable segment.

Cultural Issues

Living between China and Japan, Koreans have absorbed a great deal from their two neighbors but have nonetheless maintained a unique culture. Although Korean-Americans op-erate in the mainstream, they still have limited interaction with it. Many Korean-Americans say that they haven't made enough of an effort to integrate themselves into their new surround-ings. The values and traditions that make them succeed also insulate them from the mainstream and from other ethnics and minorities. One Korean-American business owner in Los An-geles says, "You become a small island. You don't reach out for help, you always reach in." This combination of insularity, lack of fluency in English, and Korea's history of foreign occupa-tions has sometimes resulted in cultural clashes, often within the communities that the Korean-Americans serve.

Korean culture is most visible to mainstream America through its distinct language (Han'gul) and foods. It has been shaped by various religions and philosophies, notably Bud-dhism. The first Methodist and Presbyterian missionaries ar-rived in Korea over one hundred years ago, and, although Protestantism is a minority religion in Korea, the number of Protestant churches serving Koreans in the United States began to grow in the 1970s, when waves of Koreans immigrated.

Koreans are one of the fastest-growing groups of Protestants in this country, with over four thousand churches nationwide.

U.S. Korean Protestant denominations tend to be strongly evangelical, but their churches also help recent immigrants meet other Koreans. The cultural lure of the church is very strong, and many Korean Buddhists convert when they come to the United States. Korean Protestants are usually either business owners or professionals, constituting an upscale Korean Christian segment that takes celebrating Christmas and other Christian holidays seriously.

As with other Asian-Americans, personal relationshps dominate everything. The family, the group, the work unit may be one and the same for Korean-Americans. One of the major issues about which Korean-Americans feel strongly is the lack of available time to spend with their children because of the demands of work. Marketers of educational and financial services can appeal to the concern for family that characterizes this group.

Japanese-Americans

The first American to win the Olympic gold medal in figure skating since 1976 was Kristi Yamaguchi in the 1992 Winter Olympics. Kristi, an American of Japanese descent, soon appeared on Kellogg's Special K cereal packages and endorsed other products. Commenting on her victory, one young man, quoted anonymously in *The New York Times*, hoped that it would help reduce stereotyping of Americans of Asian heritage: "We are not all math or science wizards or laundry operators or restaurant owners, but skaters, architects, writers. And more. And less. Without hyphens."

From Issei to Yonsei

Japanese-Americans, or Americans of Japanese descent, *can* do anything and have been successful for many years. Sometimes they use the Japanese terms *issei, nisei, sansei,* and *yonsei*—

meaning first-, second-, third-, and fourth-generation Americans—to describe themselves.

The first generation of Japanese came to Hawaii and to the West Coast between 1885 and 1924. (Prior to 1885, Japan didn't allow emigration.) Most of these early immigrants worked as farmers or as small-business owners. As they succeeded, they sent their children to college, producing the first generation of Japanese-American professionals in the United States.

Japanese-Americans born in the early 1940s were born into a particularly ugly time in U.S. history. In 1942, during World War II, one hundred thousand Japanese-Americans on the West Coast, even if they were U.S. citizens, were stripped of their property and isolated in internment camps, simply because they were of Japanese descent. Nonetheless, large numbers of Japanese-Americans joined the U.S. armed forces and fought in the European theater of operations.

Despite their difficult beginnings, Japanese-Americans born during these years have become quite successful. Close to 90 percent have attended college, and many are professionals. Most of them do not speak Japanese, although they would like to, and many of their elderly parents consider them "too American."

Third-generation Japanese-Americans appear highly assimilated. Most live in predominantly white neighborhoods, and a large percentage have married whites. Most would like to see the hyphen in their identity eliminated, but, despite their success and assimilation, it stands.

But that doesn't mean that Japanese-Americans have given up on the Japanese part either. Their traditions still exert a strong pull, and many are trying to reconcile them with assimilation and acculturation.

Many second-generation Japanese-Americans felt pressure from their parents to keep their traditions alive but at the same time wanted to be accepted as Americans. Approximately 50 percent of all third-generation Japanese-Americans married whites, helping to move the assimilation process along. Succeeding generations of Japanese have adopted more mainstream American behaviors and values. However, the important core values of hard work, loyalty to the group and to one's

superiors, obligation to return favors, and respect for age and
tradition are still important, in varying degrees, to most Japanese-Americans, and there is a movement among some Japanese-Americans to preserve the cultural elements of their heritage.

Education has always been a way for immigrants to the
United States to rise above their early and often lower-class
status. Few ethnic groups in general believe in the value of
education as much as the Japanese. For the Japanese in America, the drive to do well in school has had an added component;
it is a matter of honor that children excel in school—both the
family's honor and the honor of the Japanese people.

Segments and Salarymen

Of the approximately eight hundred fifty thousand Japanese-
Americans in the U.S., more than 80 percent live on the West
Coast. A small group lives on the East Coast, and a few are in
the Midwest and the South. Close to 90 percent of Japanese-
Americans were born in the United States. The median family
income is 32 percent above the national average. In the face of
the early years of discrimination and recurring episodes of so-
called Japan bashing, Japanese-Americans have been enormously successful.

On the East Coast, especially in the New York area, there
are an estimated fifty to sixty thousand Japanese "salarymen"
and their families, living there on a temporary basis. These
temporary residents are sent to the United States by their
multinational corporations for only a few years. Because of the
salarymen's strong company ties and the cultural gap between
the salarymen and other Japanese-Americans, there is little
interaction between the two groups. A third reason for the lack
of interaction is the almost universal feeling among Japanese
that those who have emigrated have turned their backs on their
heritage.

Very few of these temporary workers stay in the United
States long enough to become acculturated. Most Japanese
families stay for three or four years; only about 10 percent

remain in the United States permanently. These families tend to keep a very low profile, and there is a strong effort on their part to stay "very Japanese." But they provide an important economic stimulant for the regions where they live, and businesses in parts of Westchester County in New York and Bergen County in New Jersey that cater to temporary Japanese residents are flourishing.

Both groups of Japanese—permanent immigrants and salarymen—are very sophisticated consumers with a good deal of money to spend, even though there are fewer of them than of other Asian groups. Dr. Diane Simpson of Simpson International, New York, says, "Think purchasing power, not overall statistics, when evaluating a segment."

Quality is the key in marketing to either assimilated mainstream Americans of Japanese descent or to Japanese temporary residents. While Japanese-Americans would deeply love to see more Japanese and other Asians represented in print and TV advertising, this segment is for the most part best reached through mainstream media. Prestige labels and high-quality, reliable goods appeal to both segments.

One way for marketers to reach part of the Japanese market on the East Coast is to use Japanese-language media, such as the "Supertime" television show. "Supertime" claims that 80 percent of Japanese in the New York tri-state area watch the show and that the average household income of viewers is over $60,000.

Asian Indians

The well-being of the family is also an important issue for Asian Indians, a very diverse group that comprises almost 1 million immigrants from three different countries: India, Pakistan, and Bangladesh. Indians account for about 10 percent of Asians in the United States. This entrepreneurial segment includes many professionals, including doctors and engineers, and owners and managers of motels, gas stations, and convenience stores.

Indian Diversity

India itself is one of the most ethnically diverse countries in the world, with religion and language separating people more than ethnic background. Twenty-four languages are each spoken by more than 1 million people. But Hindi and English, along with fourteen others, are the official languages. India is 85 percent Hindu but includes many Moslems and followers of other religions. Even Indian Hinduism differs from region to region and from class to class. For example, wheat is a sacred food in the North, but rice is sacred in the South.

From the outset, Islam established itself in the region as a second culture parallelling Hinduism. Pakistan and Bangladesh are predominantly Moslem. Buddhism and Jainism, although they originated in India, are now more prevalent in the small country of Sri Lanka (formerly Ceylon), an island off the southeast coast of India.

Cultural Similarities

Despite the many differences among them, Asian Indians have many cultural traits in common. The ideal family is large, and family always takes precedence over the individual. Even in the United States, extended Asian Indian families often live together or close by. Elders are respected and cared for by their children, and divorce rates are low.

Many Asian Indians are religious and believe strongly in simple material comforts and rich spirituality. Fatalism, a component of all the major religions of India, is widespread. Humility and self-denial for the good of the group are the ideal, typified by the respected leader Mahatma Gandhi.

Many Asian Indians are vegetarians, often because of religious beliefs. All the castes (class divisions by occupation and ethnic origin) have different food laws and customs, as does each religion. Hindus consider cows to be sacred and, even if they are not vegetarians, don't eat beef. Moslems eat beef but not pork and drink no alcohol. In a marketing research study, Paul Sladkus found that many Indians prefer Pizza Hut to McDonald's, probably because many Indians are vegetarians.

My brother-in-law was born in India and came to the United States with his parents when he was sixteen. On the surface, he is very assimilated—he is a senior-level executive at one of California's most prestigious corporations. But, like many well-educated first-generation professionals, he takes great pride in certain aspects of his culture. One of the ways he expresses his pride is by cooking superb Indian food—spicy chicken and beef curries, savory lentil and vegetable stews, and garlicky vegetable fritters.

Assimilation and acculturation do not occur uniformly within Asian Indian segments. Religion, economics, intermarriage, and other variables affect the rate and extent of assimilation.

History

In the early 1900s a small number of Indians came to the United States and settled in California. They were unskilled farmers and small-business owners. Most of them were Sikhs, followers of a religion that tried to reconcile the differences between Hinduism and Islam. The Sikhs, whose then-independent state of Punjab was overcrowded and poor, began coming to the United States to find a haven from intra-Indian discrimination.

Along with this group of immigrants came students from East India who came to study at polytechnical schools and Ivy League universities. Indian students are still an important subsegment of the Asian-American market and are present on many U.S. campuses.

Asian Indians can be quite dark-skinned. Although they are racially Caucasian, they have often experienced prejudice in this country. But most Asian Indians have adapted, acculturated, and prospered.

Immigration

Since 1965, immigration from the Indian subcontinent has boomed. Between World War II and 1965, the new immigrants were mostly professionals and their families. After 1965, newer arrivals came from Bombay and Calcutta. The influx of new immigrants has spread throughout the United States, but most Indians still settle in New York and California; New York's Little Indias, in downtown Manhattan and on 74th Street in Jackson Heights, Queens, are flourishing.

Asian Indians can be reached with English-language advertising. But they often can't be reached by mainstream advertising or promotion. For example, don't expect Indians to identify with images of blond surfers. Many Indian English-languages publications are available to marketers at a fraction of the cost of mainstream media. This segment will probably grow more rapidly in the late 1990s as a result of ethnic civil strife in India during 1992 and 1993.

Other Asian-Americans

In addition to those we have discussed, other Asian groups have immigrated to the United States in substantial numbers and will continue to arrive in the near future. The Vietnamese are the largest of these groups; there are currently more than 1 million Vietnamese in the United States, accounting for about 14 percent of all Asian-Americans. Vietnamese are the third largest group of Asian-Americans and are expected to grow in number more rapidly than other groups. Cambodians and Laotians have also joined the Vietnamese who first came here after U.S. troops left Vietnam in 1973.

Since 1975, more than 2 million refugees have left Vietnam, Laos, and Cambodia and gone to China, Thailand, Hong Kong, and Malaysia. Many subsequently have come to the United States. Some have settled in suburbs, and others have joined other immigrant groups in revitalizing the inner cities.

About half of all Vietnamese in the United States have settled in California; others have stayed in different parts of the West Coast, and a fair number have made their way to the East Coast.

A growing class of educated, professional young Vietnamese-Americans is beginning to flex its political and purchasing power. Many Vietnamese-Americans feel a conflict between traditional values and assimilation. One Vietnamese refugee, speaking in *The New York Times* about the impact of U.S. culture on first-generation Vietnamese-Americans, said, "Our Vietnamese culture is of steel, but yours is acid that dissolves the steel." A Vietnamese bilingual teacher says, "The older generation doesn't want to assimilate, but the younger generation does. The older folks fear that young people will lose their Vietnamese identity."

There are many Vietnamese who are young, poor, and poorly educated, and the median family income of Vietnamese-Americans is lower than that of other Asian-Americans. Vietnamese also have more family members per household than other Asian groups. But this subgroup is growing faster than any other Asian segment. It is estimated that there will be more than 1.5 million Vietnamese in the United States by 2000. Southern California is home to about two thousand Vietnamese small businesses and the community there seems to be expanding rapidly.

Reaching the Vietnamese market is somewhat more difficult than reaching Chinese-Americans, but the numbers make it well worth the effort, especially because of the rapid growth of the Vietnamese segment.

One company that sells baby pictures works in conjunction with more than 2,000 hospitals around the country. When the field force reported an influx of Vietnamese in Wichita, Kansas, the company had all its support materials and brochures translated into Vietnamese. In California and New York, in-language ad agencies and consultants can advise marketers on how to reach this fast-growing segment.

An estimated 25,000 to 30,000 Cambodians live in California; it is said that there are more Cambodian restaurants in greater San Francisco than in any other city in the world, including the Cambodian capital of Phnom Penh.

In addition to Vietnamese and Cambodians, Indonesians, Thais, and other Asians (totaling about 1 million) account for a growing market. These groups are still too small to segment out, but be aware that Asian-Americans respond with great purchasing power when marketers do their part to reach out to them. Just acknowledging their existence can provide a large group of brand- and company-loyal consumers.

A Note on Hawaii

Hawaii is a special case and a very special state. It is home not only to beautiful palm trees, sunshine, and surf, but to the only majority nonwhite population among the fifty states. More than 65 percent of the residents claim Asian or Pacific Island descent. That majority includes ethnic Chinese, Japanese, Filipinos, and others, as well as native Hawaiians. There are around 1.25 million people on the islands, and the population is growing.

Many Hawaiians tell us not to try to segment the Hawaiian market along ethnic lines. Paul Brewbaker, an economist at the Bank of Hawaii, says, in *Sales and Marketing Management* magazine, "Everybody here considers themselves American. People's ethnic and cultural roots aren't strong enough to overcome the impact of homogenization. Even if we wanted to segment a market along racial lines, it wouldn't be a worthwhile step because the census is all screwed up."

Statistics are often fairly inaccurate and can confuse an already sticky issue. For example, many Hawaiians are of mixed ancestry. Robert C. Schmitt, a statistician for the Hawaii Department of Business and Economic Development, says that his in-laws, who are part Hawaiian and part Chinese, responded differently to the census—some said they were Hawaiian, and some said Chinese.

Despite the impossibility of subsegmenting Hawaiians accurately by their ethnicity, some marketers do note certain ethnic differences. There is enough homogeneity to design a general market campaign, but it is very important to take into account the nuances that matter to different segments.

Listen to Claudia Schmidt, senior vice president at Starr Seigle McCombs, a Honolulu advertising agency, also speaking in *Sales and Marketing Management* magazine: "If, for example, you're marketing automobiles, you wouldn't craft a different campaign for, say, Japanese and Chinese. But you do need to be aware that the preferred method of paying off a car will vary: The Chinese tend to pay in cash and hold onto the car a long time. The Japanese, on the other hand, will finance the purchases. So, although you wouldn't do a separate campaign, you would need to emphasize a broad range of financing choices."

One of Hawaiians' chief complaints is that they feel that marketers are simply ignoring Hawaiians. The main thrust of marketing, they feel, is toward tourists. Otherwise, Hawaiians say, marketers treat Hawaii as an afterthought and assume that if it works in California, it'll work in Hawaii. But there are well over a million consumers in Hawaii who would love to be our loyal customers, if we just do our part to acknowledge their purchasing power.

An Interview With William Orton, Metropolitan Life Insurance Company

This chapter's interview is with William Orton, Director of Target Marketing for Met Life.

Q: *Please talk about your background, how you got to this point, and your position here at Metropolitan Life.*

WO: My position today is Director of Target Marketing. That includes our activities within the ethnic markets, as well as developing target marketing programs for the force at large. I've been with Met Life for twenty-one years.

Q: *Please talk about the background or history of Metropolitan Life and its position. And, if you can, discuss who are your major competitors.*

WO: Metropolitan Life will be celebrating its one hundred twenty-fifth anniversary next year. It is not the oldest, but it is one of the oldest life insurance companies. In terms of its asset size, it is exceeded in size only by Prudential. In essence we're the second largest insurance company in the United States. We operate through a distribution system that consists of a little over thirteen thousand sales reps spread out through the United States, who report to more than sixty different regional offices.

Q: *Can you discuss the evolution of your marketing program, particularly for the Asian market segment?*

WO: We began formally in the Asian market back in the early 1980's, when we began looking at the changing demographics and the changing American population. We thought there was an opportunity for us that we could expand upon, that we weren't serving that segment of the market as well as we could.

We began back then—our field force was much smaller than it is today. And we began by talking to them and getting an assessment of the market, doing our own research into the size of the market and where it was located. A lot of our effort was in educating our own field management team—the people in the branches and regional offices throughout the country—about the opportunity out there that they ought to pursue.

Q: *How do you see your marketing programs for ethnic segments differing from your mainstream marketing programs?*

WO: We use essentially the same types of agents. They have the same contracts, they work out of the same office structure. Primarily, they are of the same ethnic background as the market we are serving.

The product line is the same. What we have done to make the market grow is essentially to create awareness of it for people who are responsible for the sales and marketing at the local level, and two, to do a lot of work in terms of translations so that we have materials sales reps can use sitting down with people and explaining our products and services in the language they are most comfortable in.

Q: *Is the message the same?*

WO: The message is essentially the same. We have changed the message in some respects to reflect some of the interests of our reps and the market, but they are really slight changes. One of the biggest difficulties is just in the plain translation, the direct translation, making sure the message you are conveying doesn't get taken too far out of context. The one mistake you try to avoid is conveying the wrong message.

And there is not always a direct literal translation from English to Chinese, for example. So, in that respect, most of the differences [in the message] vary [because of the] translation process. In addition to that, anything we translate we send out to a group of advisers we have in our field force to make sure that translated message is in keeping with how we want to position that product or service with the client base.

Q: *How do you create awareness, how do you target, how do you reach? How did you really research this particular market? You indicated earlier that you had feedback from your sales reps. Is that a major source of your market research?*

WO: It's an important source. I would divide our market intelligence into two areas. There's that area where we already have a strong base. For example, in the metropolitan area, we have a very strong group of Asian managers and sales reps who are doing an excellent job of pursuing the market. In that case we don't need to rely on demographics to tell us where the market is—it's very visible.

We do rely on our account reps in those instances to keep us abreast of changes in the market, their perception of how well our Asian advertising is doing, for example, what some of our competitors are doing—because they're out in the street every day.

The other part of our market intelligence is in those areas where ethnic populations have grown rather quickly and we're not taking advantage of them. There we rely on some demographics and census data in starting to pinpoint and identify the opportunity for field managers.

Q: *Do you find a lot of business is gotten by word of mouth?*

WO: Within the Asian market, a lot of it is very much people I know. It is not done, for example, in a direct-mail type of solicitation. It doesn't work in that market. "Eight-hundred"-type numbers don't work in that market. If I had to state what the differences are, it is probably much more of a personal contact market, a referral, relationship market, than the general market—but only by a matter of degrees.

Q: *Is it dependent on the amount of assimilation or what a particular segment or customer may have been exposed to?*

WO: If we look at the most recent immigrant market, people who have recently come into the country and are still first-generation and have not totally assimilated, our successful agents in that market provide services and help far beyond the traditional insurance roles. They will help people with all sorts of business and financial problems—finding a way to do anything, like getting a driver's license or getting a car registered. If they are successful, those successful reps tend to be almost full-service advisers to the people they are working with, which is important in establishing that trust and connection.

Q: *How do you build awareness, interest, and action in that particular segment? Does it relate back to word of mouth and relationships?*

WO: We also have done things corporately. When we began the program, one of the things we identified that we had to do was create some name recognition for the company. We couldn't rely on our corporate advertising to be recognized and to single us out in that particular market segment. We had to look toward media that were directed at the Asian community, for example.

And our message was initially just to get across a sense of who we were as a company and to convey the values that we perceived the Asian community was looking for—that we were financially strong, that we were a large company, that we have a long tradition of integrity and strength.

Q: What do you think mainstream companies need to do to succeed in ethnic targeted segments?

WO: Well, one of the first things they have to do is recognize that it's there, recognize that it's an opportunity. They have to recognize that being a mainstream company is not going to work for you anymore, because that mainstream that got you to where you are today is getting smaller. That was one of the things that Metropolitan Life Insurance looked at ten or fifteen years ago.

They realized that the traditional life insurance market, which was a husband and wife with two kids and a mortgage, is not today what America is about. There are a lot of diverse cultures and family situations. And you have to start identifying them within both the mainstream and the ethnic markets.

Q: After the identification, what other nuances or strategies do mainstream companies need to use or learn to be successful in ethnic marketing?

WO: Well, you do have to learn that there are cultural differences. Or you have to be aware of cultural differences. You work with ethnic advertising firms, for example. Ethnic marketing consultants and your own field force, once they get established, can be your ultimate ethnic experts, because they are meeting the clients every day.

Are there differences in the marketing strategies? Yes, but they are probably more nuances than major differences. For us, though, it's recognizing that you have to have the same ethnic mix or cultural mix in your distribution system as the market you are pursuing. You can't have an all-white, male field force and expect to be successful marketing to Asians, or Hispanics, or African-Americans, or women. As a company, you need to reflect the world around you. That may seem obvious.

Q: *What do you see as some of the opportunities in this specific segment?*

WO: If you look at population trends over the next ten years, ethnic groups collectively are expected to generate more than 60 percent of the population growth. So the opportunities that we have now are only going to become bigger and greater. We probably really only skim the surface in terms of pursuing various ethnic and cultural groups in the United States. There are people moving in from Eastern Europe in greater and greater numbers. There's a Russian market, and it's one that we're starting to look at, and we've actually made some progress in different areas.

A lot of what you learn from one market is transferable. Yes, there are cultural differences between all of them. But the process is pretty much the same for us. We find out where they live or where there is a concentrated population. We obtain a profile—age, income, and demographics. We work with the local manager to try to stimulate and create interest from our people and from the manager pursuing that market and creating interest in Met Life in that market. We are here, and we are an interested member of that community—both that we offer job opportunities and that we offer some very valuable services.

Q: *What do you see as some of the challenges in pursuing an ethnic market segment?*

WO: For any ethnic segment, once you get involved, you realize that there are a whole bunch of things you could be doing. You could be doing a lot of advertising, you could be participating in a lot of community events. You could be translating all of your sales material into a particular language.

Your real challenge in any market is how you apply limited resources to it. And there it comes down to decisions about where we would get more benefit—by participating in a community event or by advertising. These are those types of challenges that you have to be aware of.

I'll give you an example. In the Asian Indian market, there is no need to translate. It is a predominantly English-speaking community. There are also a number of Indian dialects. Once you start translating, there's just no end. In the Asian market, you have to be aware of the difference between Cantonese and Mandarin. So you have to be aware of what area of origin a particular Chinese community comes from.

Q: *Is your involvement in ethnic marketing viewed as part of marketing operations or as a corporate or social responsibility? You do acknowledge a greater return on investment, don't you?*

WO: No, it's not done out of a corporate or social responsibility requirement. We do have a corporate responsibility area, the Met Life Foundation. They do marvelous work supporting a wide variety of causes. They contribute to Asian communities and African-American communities, and we are aware of that here in marketing. But it's not a coordinated effort, or one used directly in our marketing efforts. If we're dealing with a community leader in a market, we'll convey that we are a supporter of the community. It is part of the overall image of the company, but it's not something we wave a flag at. What we are doing in marketing is not driven by that. There is certainly a good return on investment, more than anything else.

6

Marketing to African-Americans

On vacation in St. Thomas, in the U.S. Virgin Islands, a few years ago, I watched a young mother slather her small sons with sunscreen. This is hardly an unusual sight today. When I was a child, no one knew that children's delicate skin burned even more severely than adult skin, and kids were sent out into the sun unprotected to "get their Vitamin D." But today, few people today let their youngsters play on a burning beach without sun protection. So I was surprised to hear a woman, while looking at the heavily lotioned children, whisper to her companion, "I didn't know that black people needed sunscreen."

Black people, of course, can burn severely, just as whites do. The ignorance about blacks among some members of the white population is surprising, but not as surprising as the ignorance on the part of some marketers. If profit is the objective of all companies, why not explore all options? For example, why hasn't Coppertone ever shown a black child in its famous ad?

Myth No. 1: All Blacks Are Poor

The sun protection lotion story illustrates just one of the myths surrounding marketing to African-Americans. One of the most pervasive myths is that almost all blacks are poor, so it's not worth targeting them. Of course, there are poor African-Americans; many studies show that poor blacks are poorer today than before. According to the Census Bureau, around 60 percent of black households in 1990 had incomes of less than $25,000, compared to 40 percent of white households. However, only about one third of blacks are poor; two thirds are above the Census Bureau's poverty threshold index for 1991.*

Studies also show that the middle- and upper-income segments of the black community have grown enormously in the past ten years. More than 13 percent of households headed by blacks have incomes of $50,000 or more. And, in this highly segmented market, even people with lower incomes buy and use goods and services.

One of the reasons that poverty is such an issue is visibility. Poor blacks are concentrated in densely populated urban areas, making them highly visible. Although blacks make up less than 30 percent of poor Americans, they constitute more than 40 percent of the poor in central cities.

Affluent blacks, in contrast, are far less visible. In 1990 there were forty U.S. metropolitan areas that included at least 50,000 black suburbanites. That doesn't mean that everyone in the suburbs is rich, but living in the suburbs often implies home ownership and a measure of prosperity for those 75 percent of suburbanites who are above the poverty line. Even of the half of all African-Americans who live in the central cities, close to two thirds are not poor.

The black middle class and upper middle class, moreover, are increasingly affluent, educated, and professional. A study done by the U.S. Bureau of Labor Statistics on black progress in the professions and in business between 1972 and 1991 showed gains of up to 470 percent in areas such as accounting, engineering, computer programming, law, medicine, journalism, and management.

*The Census Bureau set the household poverty line in 1991 as : one person, $6,932; two people, $8,865; three people, $10,860; four people, $13,924; and five people, $16,456.

Blacks in Corporate America

Blacks have seen rapid changes in how they are accepted in business, which has historically been more resistant than the professions to women and minorities. According to a February 1992 *Black Enterprise* magazine review of U.S. corporations, many high-level positions were held by African-Americans. Federal Express Corporation of Memphis, Tennessee, had 13 percent of its management slots filled by African-Americans, as did the Equitable Insurance Company of New York. Ten percent of the managers at General Motors in Detroit were black, as were 18 percent of managers and more than 13 percent of senior managers at McDonald's in Oak Brook, Illinois.

Most black-owned businesses are small, but the nation's one hundred largest black businesses posted gains of more than 10 percent even in recessionary 1991, with sales totaling over $7.2 billion. Los Angeles and New York each had more than 20,000 black-owned businesses, followed by Washington, D.C., and Chicago, with nearly as many.

The $300 Billion Market

For every black celebrity and superstar we can name, there are hundreds of successful and creative African-Americans who are not household names. When we look at black America, we are looking at a total market of almost 32 million people, with close to $300 billion in spending power.

African-Americans are a large and growing market, representing more than 12 percent of the total U.S. population. And this is a unique market. Even though blacks are making more and more money, they aren't becoming more like white consumers. According to Al Anderson, president of his own Atlanta communications firm, "Black people aren't dark-skinned white people. Their core doesn't change." For Mr. Anderson, the formula for marketing to blacks consists of relevance, recognition, and respect. "The fourth 'R' is results—

what you get when you follow this formula," says Mr. Anderson.

Denise Gardner, marketing vice president of Soft Sheen beauty products, says in *Marketing News* that "the black consumer weighs who you are and what do you mean to me." She adds (in an observation reminiscent of what Avon's Sonia Green says about the way Hispanic women view shopping), "African-American women are avid consumers" who still enjoy a shopping spree in a time when "dislike for shopping among the general population is at an all-time high. Black women use shopping as a social occasion."

In fact, it's not only black women who are avid consumers. According to a 1993 study by Yankelovich Partners and Burrell Communications Group, 56 percent of blacks say they enjoy clothes shopping, compared to 29 percent of other consumers. Other surveys show that African-Americans buy 16 percent of the orange juice and 36 percent of the hair conditioning products sold in America. And blacks spend a greater portion of their incomes on apparel, footwear, and home electronics than does the general market, according to *Sales and Marketing Management* magazine.

According to *American Demographics* magazine, blacks account for 10 percent of expenditures on televisions, radios, and sound equipment. Blacks also account for 17 percent of expenditures on encyclopedias and other reference books. Some black parents say that, because their education was cut short, they want the reference books for their children so they can better answer their questions. Other parents simply want their children to have the best educational materials available to them.

Like many immigrant groups, African-Americans realize that knowledge is power, and they encourage their children to get a good education. Dr. Henry Louis Gates, Jr., the W. E. B. Du Bois professor of the Humanities at Harvard, wrote eloquently in *Forbes* magazine that when he was a child, he was told thousands of times to "get as much education as you can, boy; nobody can take your education away from you."

If you reach out to the African-American market with respect and relevance and cultivate ongoing relationships, you will see a greater return on your marketing dollar than you will with the general market. Larry Glover, executive vice president of J. Curtis & Company of Montclair, New Jersey, says, "African-Americans feel neglected—they're prime purchasers of branded products. They're loyal but also willing to try new products, and advertisers were not inviting them into the consumer franchise."

Blacks are not uniformly brand-loyal. They are a highly subsegmented and stratified market. Many upscale African-Americans buy private-label and generic goods, which are less expensive than brand names. The proliferation of discount and cut-price stores and warehouse clubs has popularized generics and bulk buying.

Paradoxically, less affluent African-Americans tend to buy fewer generic goods, possibly because generics don't have the status of branded goods, because blacks may be unaware of them, or because generic products are unavailable to them. Name brands still report higher consumption levels among most ethnics and minorities than do follower brands.

Whether it is the poverty myth, the fear of venturing into an unknown market, or just plain ignorance that holds back mainstream marketers, the fact is that not enough goods and services are being targeted to the African-American market and its segments. Many businesses that are struggling to stay afloat continue to target the same overtapped general market when going after black consumers could make the difference between breaking even and increased market share and profit.

Something as simple as replacing a traditional white Santa Claus with a black Santa at South DeKalb Mall in Atlanta increased sales of Santa items by 51 percent. The South DeKalb Mall restyled itself as an Afrocentric retail mall and found its profits increasing. Even the 1991 Christmas catalog was targeted to black consumers. Here was something African-Americans could identify with—a smiling black Santa carrying two beautiful little girls. It wasn't any wonder that the campaign succeeded.

It seems hard to understand, especially in recessionary times, why companies still seem to resist reaching out to the black (or for that matter, any nonmainstream) consumer market. Although African-Americans have traditionally bought American-made cars, today many are buying foreign cars. Yet few foreign-car companies advertise to African-Americans. Honda is a notable exception. It advertises to blacks with the patriotic theme "Made in Marysville, Ohio, by American workers." The ad agencies are simply not getting the word out to their foreign automotive clients that blacks should be targeted, too.

Pepper and Ronald Miller, president and vice president, respectively, of P. Hunter & Associates in Chicago, writing in *Marketing News*, find that marketers are inexperienced in targeting African-Americans. Today, for example, many blacks are looking for financial services and financial planning. The Millers say that African-Americans are more cautious about their investments than are mainstream consumers. So, companies that can provide special investment programs will find great opportunities in this market, and promotional campaigns that educate and foster confidence and reassurance will work well.

Financial services giants like Fidelity, which sells mutual funds, reach out to blacks with television ads. MassMutual Life Insurance shows a smiling black child with his handsome father in some of its print ads. And Allstate Insurance now uses black hands in its "good hands" spots. Most financial services companies, however, still ignore the growing dollar power of the African-American market.

A glaring example of missed opportunity stood out in an issue of *Ebony* magazine. The magazine ran an article on heart-healthy meals; the recipes included called for items like skim milk, unsalted chicken broth, and low-fat cottage cheese. This isn't surprising; most people are concerned with better diet, and African-Americans suffer disproportionately from hypertension (high blood pressure).

What is surprising is that in that issue of the magazine, there wasn't a single ad for low-salt or low-fat products. There were the usual ads for soft drinks, beer, and fast-food restaurants, but not one marketer of heart-healthy foods took advantage of this huge, untapped market.

Ebony did a large part of the job by creating awareness and educating the consumer. However, mainstream marketers need to be aware of these opportunities and to capitalize on them by advertising in *Ebony* and other high-circulation publications.

Another area that is ignored by mainstream companies is the black travel-for-pleasure market. Pepper and Ronald Miller say that African-Americans are spending a great deal of money on domestic and overseas trips, especially to places where they have historical roots, such as Africa and the Caribbean. Yet few agencies, tour operators, franchisers, airlines, or cruise lines make the effort to target this group. Other high-growth areas for the African-American market include health care, credit cards, health and beauty aids, and retailing.

The Millers agree that African-Americans have historically been brand-loyal. But now, they say, blacks listen, watch, and evaluate ad information before making the decision to buy. They stress that African-Americans are less likely to buy or trust products that are not advertised. Despite these facts, little or no advertising is aimed directly at blacks.

Myth No. 2: The Same Ads Can Reach Both Blacks and Whites

A second myth is that blacks and whites can be reached through the same ads and the same media. The truth is that to succeed with African-Americans, ads must be relevant to their lifestyle and must reflect a positive image of them as consumers.

Some marketers suggest that they can reach African-Americans through general-market publications. Eugene Morris, president of E. Morris, Ltd., a Chicago ad agency, disagrees. He notes that blacks may account for only 10 to 12 percent of a mass-market publication's readership.

Larry Glover goes a step further. He believes that companies continue to believe in the myth that, because black people speak English, they can be reached through general market publications.

Greg Walker, marketing communications manager for Eastman Kodak, says, "The temptation in the past has been to think that an African-American audience or a nonwhite audience is not so distinctly different or difficult to reach or that the use of a well-known celebrity will automatically make for an ethnic marketing effort. That is the one-size-fits-all approach to marketing, and we know that doesn't work."

The "add-on-a-black-celebrity" approach to a mainstream campaign rarely succeeds unless it takes into account the broader set of variables that needs to be considered when selling to black consumers. According to the study by Yankelovich Partners and Burrell Communications Group, 60 percent of black consumers feel that most television and print ads "are designed only for white people."

Most companies analyze historical data, come up with a marketing plan, and then figure out how to implement the plan. Larry Glover says this is a mistake when attempting to target the African-American market. He feels that "black media need to be brought in during planning so that when you get to execution, it's clear what impact all the execution will have." And some industry experts suggest that using a black ad agency can prevent public relations problems.

Not every product and service needs to have a separate marketing campaign dedicated to the black consumer. As with global marketing, the overall marketing strategy can be standard, but the promotional mix must be tailored for the specific market. Advertising, promotion, publicity, and selling must be carefully adjusted for the specific segments of the target.

Black Media

Advertising in black media is somewhat less expensive than advertising in mass media, and the higher return on investment always justifies the outlay. There are almost 800 black media outlets (print, radio, and TV) from which to choose. Given that number, marketing organizations could never say that they can't find appropriate vehicles for reaching the African-American audience.

Cable television's Black Entertainment Television network (BET) reaches close to 55 percent of black households and is watched by an audience that is 89 percent black. And in the recessionary years of the early 1990s, while U.S. television advertising was up just a small percentage, minority advertising was up significantly. BET registered a gain of 20 percent in 1991, most of the revenue coming from existing clients. (There was, however, a decrease in the number of new clients.)

Blacks listen to the radio the equivalent of about one day per week. Advertisers can save a lot of money by reaching blacks via radio because the listening audience is segmented in fewer ways than the white audience. For example, to reach Chicago's eighteen-to-thirty-five-year-old general audience, advertisers must buy time on at least five stations, compared to two or three stations to reach a similar black segment. And the rates on these stations are lower than for the "white" stations.

Print is also an excellent way to reach black segments. More than 70 percent of African-Americans read community-based news publications. *Essence* magazine reaches 4 million readers; no other single women's magazine has a 25 percent penetration rate. Although a good number of black women read *Vogue* and *Mademoiselle*, for many black women, *Essence* is "home." Black executives may read *Forbes*, *Fortune*, and *Business Week*, but many also read *Black Enterprise*.

In an effort to increase unit sales, the publishers of *Ebony*, *Essence*, *Black Enterprise*, *Black Elegance*, *Emerge*, and *YSB* have banded together to place their publications in more than three thousand displays near the impulse-purchase zone at checkout counters. This spot had traditionally been filled by magazines that bought slots chainwide, which even the biggest black publications couldn't afford to do on their own. The black magazine publishers believed that their titles belonged in stores with significant black traffic, not just in black neighborhoods. Their efforts have been paying off.

Inclusive Advertising

Advertising in black media should be only a part of your strategy. Some companies are showing ads in mainstream media featuring blacks and whites; this can be very effective with products that are "universals"—that are used in the same way and for the same benefits by most people. Procter and Gamble's Scope mouthwash television commercial, for example, features a white woman, a white man, and a black man, all shown humorously avoiding their significant other's kiss until they've gargled. The actors are nice-looking, ordinary, thirtyish to fortyish, all spirited and adorable, especially at the end of the commercial, when they're ready for their kiss.

Some critics argue that there are still too few blacks in ads and that when blacks are shown, they are depicted in downscale or stereotypic occupations, such as janitors or athletes. Worse, they say, blacks are put in nonthreatening or subordinate positions in order to avoid scaring off the general market.

In a report called "Still Invisible," done by the New York City Department of Consumer Affairs, more than 2,100 ads from ten magazines, from *Better Homes and Gardens* to *Vogue*, were surveyed. Blacks appeared in only 3.4 percent of national magazine ads and 4.6 percent of mail-order catalogs, even though blacks account for more than 11 percent of the readership of all magazines. For those companies that are afraid of using black models in mainstream advertising, some studies have shown that white audiences react positively to black models in ads. One ad in a business magazine showed a little girl with her sleeve rolled up, bravely awaiting her vaccine from the doctor standing next to her. The copy talked about physician referrals and regional health-care databases. Sound like the usual business-to-business ad? It was, except that the doctor was black and the little girl was white. Similarly, American Express ran an ad in several mainstream business magazines for its Optima card, which showed a black family picking out plants in a greenhouse.

Many African-Americans are reached through general market media. But the multiplier effect created when black consumers see a black lifestyle print or television ad at the same time they see a general market ad for the same product in mainstream media is phenomenal. The consumer can identify with the black-directed ad and will doubly appreciate the company and its products when he or she sees that same company's ads in the mainstream media. That appreciation translates into buying behavior.

Distinct Preferences

Like all ethnic groups, blacks have some distinct preferences. For example, when blacks drink coffee, they often prefer larger helpings of sugar, cream, or nondairy creamer. Smart marketer CoffeeMate took note of this preference and began advertising in *Ebony* and *Essence* magazines, on black radio, and through outdoor ads in black neighborhoods. It also offered local sweepstakes promotions. All these steps generated tremendous increases in sales volume and market share.

The desire for sweets is pretty much universal, but blacks enjoy something sweet with their meals even more often than whites. According to the 1990 Consumer Expenditure Survey, a typical black household spends more than 50 percent more than the average white household on sugar each year.

African-Americans who smoke often prefer menthol cigarettes to plain ones. When they drink liquor, they're more likely to drink cognac than whites are. And when buying soft drinks, blacks prefer sixteen-ounce and two-liter containers to cans and other sizes, because of their family size, the lower unit price, or their lack of storage space for 6-packs and 24-unit cases.

Black consumers sometimes use products differently from the general market consumer. The Carnation Company was surprised that blacks were drinking so much of its Instant Breakfast drink. (The powder is usually mixed with milk to make a complete low-calorie breakfast.) Because African-Americans consume fewer diet products than whites, Carnation wanted to learn why their product was so popular. They found that some consumers were drinking the product and also eating a full breakfast, simply because they liked the taste of the Instant Breakfast drink.

Targeting African-Americans Through Television

Like Hispanics, African-Americans watch more television than the general population, but the viewing mix is very different. A study of Nielsen data compiled by the New York ad agency

BBDO showed that none of the ten programs most watched by blacks were on the list of the ten shows most watched by the general market. (Most of the ten shows preferred by blacks were by and/or about blacks.)

When the BBDO report on the first half of the 1992–1993 season came out, four of the top-ten shows among blacks were produced by NBC and five, by Fox. Fox spokesman James Gerber says that his network has identified the power of the black and Hispanic markets. Smart companies like Ford have capitalized on these networks' reach. During Black History Month in February 1993, Ford ads profiled not cars but largely unknown African-Americans who were outstanding in their professions.

Same Ad, Different Message

Eugene Morris, writing in *American Demographics* magazine, says that black Americans see the same ads and promotions as everyone else but that they don't always interpret them in the same way. They can come away with a negative impression even if the sponsor's intent was positive. Sometimes, blacks feel that commercial messages are so irrelevant to their lifestyle that the ads are simply ignored.

In a study conducted at DePaul University in Chicago, four commercials were viewed both by black and by white consumers. The black audience saw more deeply into the ads than did the white participants. According to the study, "Whites fail to realize certain social, respect, and accomplishment values present in some advertising. An important aspect of the black experience [is the] struggle for fulfillment, belonging, accomplishment, and respect in a white-dominated culture." Pepper Miller says that "inexperience with the African-American market and limited information cause marketers to disregard cultural- and value-based ad messages that are so critical reaching the market."

Ads that contain overt slurs would be laughable if they weren't so awful. One rice company used the image of an 1880s riverboat in a campaign aimed at black and Hispanic customers, never thinking about the negative historical associations that this image would have for many blacks. Another agency proposed an ad that would have had a black athlete saying, "Feets, don't fail me now"—a line originally associated with a stereotyped black movie character in the 1930s. Fortunately, the ad was rejected. And, at last, Quaker Oats has changed the hokey image of Aunt Jemima to make her look like a modern homemaker.

It's not such a long time ago that overt racism was the order of the day. The civil rights movement and the resulting advances in education and economic opportunities are recent phenomena. The heritage of racism still affects the way blacks view whites and themselves, as well as the way whites relate to blacks.

There's still a lot of hostility and resentment on all sides, and fingerpointing by all. But our job is to be successful marketers—to make money for companies and for ourselves. Marketers must of course consider ethics—promoting social responsibility, equality, and justice—but our primary task is to increase profit margins. So it's mind-boggling that so many companies continue to ignore the potential gold of the black consumer.

On the other hand, while too many marketers simply ignore black consumers, some companies that aim at the downscale segment have learned their marketing lessons very well—far too well, for many. Marketers of liquors, cigarettes, and high-alcohol malt liquors have targeted urban black youth and succeeded fabulously. (Blacks buy 32 percent of all malt liquor sold in the United States.)

In 1991 brewer G. Heilman planned to introduce Powermaster, an especially high-alcohol malt liquor aimed at urban blacks, but the company backed off after widespread public outcry. (It has also been criticized by some Native American activists for its high-alcohol Crazy Horse malt liquor, whose name, these critics charge, perpetuates negative stereotypes.)

A similar outcry was heard when RJR Nabisco was preparing to launch its Uptown cigarettes, aimed at the black community. The brand was scuttled after everyone from the U.S. surgeon general on down protested.

Others—black and white—are uncomfortable with current efforts to shield the black community from alcohol, tobacco, and other controversial products. Edward Lewis, the publisher of *Essence* magazine, says, "For someone to say that we cannot make up our own minds is condescending. All advertising exploits all consumers, but it gives them choices and information and allows them to make decisions." Donny Deutsch, an ad executive whose company created a controversial ad for Colt 45 malt liquor, agrees. Speaking in *The Wall Street Journal*, he says, "It reeks of paternalism and racism to suggest it is inappropriate. Why should Colt 45 shy away from portraying its core consumers just because more than 90 percent are male and black?"

To counter charges of exploitation, G. Heilman donated 10 cents to the United Negro College Fund for each case of its beer sold during Black History Month. And some tobacco companies underwrite the annual Harlem Week festival in New York. One wise black radio talk show host has sensibly asked why computer companies don't spend the same millions targeting inner city youth.

Myth No. 3: Willie Horton or Bill Cosby

Many members of the black middle class are highly educated and privileged, and they live worlds apart from the poor, inner-city underclass. Yet there is a pervasive myth that blacks are all the same and that therefore there's no need to segment them. The variation on this theme is that all blacks are either like the highly successful entertainer Bill Cosby or the notorious murderer Willie Horton, with no middle class in between.

Just as in the general market, there is a great variety in lifestyle across different geographic and psychographic segments in the African-American market. Certainly, marketers familiar with geodemographics understand that black subsegments are as varied as white ones. Just as in the mainstream, African-American geodemographic subsegments range all the way from the upscale Pools and Patios to the downmarket Hard

Scrabble, as the database from market research company Claritas Corp. describes two of its zip-code clusters.

Within the general-market middle class, there are many subsegments; even at the same income levels, people have different preferences and buying behaviors based on demographics and lifestyle. A $40,000-a-year skilled factory worker who drives a pickup truck and goes to Las Vegas on vacation is very different from a $40,000-a-year accountant in Seattle who goes to espresso bars.

Within the black middle class, there are similar lifestyle and psychographic segments. Although many blacks were thrilled when the South DeKalb Mall was redesigned to emphasize Afrocentricity, others were less enthusiastic. An Atlanta government official who lives less than two miles from the mall goes there only to get his prescriptions filled and to buy toothpaste. He complains that the stores sell the "ethnic variety" clothes that he can't wear to work, because his job requires grey-suited conformity.

Some members of the black lower class are most responsive to marketing campaigns that stress images of black unity and Afrocentric identity over all other issues. On the other hand, middle-class and upscale African-Americans' increased pride in black culture is not usually a major factor in their purchasing decisions.

While no one is suggesting that marketers need to prepare separate marketing campaigns for every single subsegment, we should at least be aware of the range of segments in the African-American market.

Demographics and Regions

The African-American market will increase to about 38 million individuals by 2010, up from about 32 million in 1993, according to the Urban Institute. Black baby boomers will continue to dominate the black population into the first decade of the twenty-first century.

Middle- and upper-class African-American boomers present the same "middle aging" marketing opportunities as do white boomers; they have the same concerns about health, retirement and financial security, college costs, and staying healthy and vital. These boomers' needs may be the same as those of the mainstream boomer market, but to capture their business, you need specifically targeted ads in black media.

Most blacks live in heavily populated areas such as Chicago, Los Angeles, New York, Detroit, and other large cities. Other areas with high concentrations of blacks are New Orleans, the Norfolk-Virginia Beach-Newport News, Virginia area, and Washington, D.C.

Close to half of all affluent black households (those with household income of more than $50,000 a year) are located in the South; the other half is spread throughout the rest of the country. In a study cited by *American Demographics* magazine and based on statistics from the Population Studies Center at the University of Michigan, fully 20 percent of blacks in Washington, D.C., were affluent. In addition, there were many affluent blacks in New York, Houston, San Francisco, and Los Angeles.

In Nassau and Suffolk counties (both suburbs of New York City), approximately 16 percent of blacks are affluent. Many southern suburban areas also have high concentrations of middle-income African-Americans. More than a quarter of the residents are black in the suburbs of Fayetteville, North Carolina; Jackson, Mississippi; Charleston and Columbia, South Carolina; and Augusta, Georgia. Many of these southern suburban blacks are affluent. Atlanta has emerged as the dynamic center of a young African-American business and professional power bloc. These "influentials" and other subsegments in the region are desirable targets for marketers.

African-American Families

Like Hispanic families, the more than 7 million black families in the United States are larger and younger than white families. In about 25 percent of white families, the head of the household is under thirty-five, compared to about 33 percent of black families. The average size of white families is about 3.1 persons, compared to almost 3.5 for blacks.

In 1990 the median income for black married couples was $34,000, compared to $40,000 for whites. The gap is narrowing, however; in populous Queens, one of the larger boroughs of New York City, for example, blacks have reached economic parity with whites.

However, there are differences between black and white families. More than half (58 percent) of the nation's black children were living with one parent in 1991, compared to only 20 percent of white children. Census Bureau data show that, in 1991, more than 31 percent of black men ages thirty-five to thirty-nine had never been married, up from 18.5 percent in 1980, and that 25 percent of black men ages twenty-five to seventy-four were not living with a spouse, a parent, or children. In 1992, among black men fifteen and older, forty-five percent had never been married, compared to 28 percent of whites.

These demographic statistics shouldn't be ignored. Chuck Morrison, president of the Morrison Group in Atlanta and a former vice president for African-American and Hispanic marketing at Coca-Cola, speaking at the 1992 American Marketing Association's Ethnic Marketing Seminar in New York, pointed out that marketers are often out of touch with reality when designing advertising strategy and copy.

Mr. Morrison cited the example of a car company whose $140 million ad campaign was being reviewed in an ad industry magazine. "It occurred to me that in the last twenty-five years, I had probably bought seventeen cars. And they were not that company's cars. I never bought one of those cars, never even considered buying one. And I started wondering why I had never purchased one of their cars: their strategy of positioning their car by advertising that 'this is not your father's you-know-what.'

"That's been their strategy for—how long?—the last five or six years? Well, I don't know who my father was. I was an illegitimate child. Fifty-four percent of black households are headed by females. So I said to myself, I wonder if they have really researched the black consumer market. Black consumer purchases of automobiles are 21 percent versus only 16 percent by whites—we buy more frequently even though we have less money. But if they were positioning themselves for the black segment they should have said, 'This is not your *mother's* you-know what.' "

Mr. Morrison and the other senior black executives I interviewed uniformly expressed confusion and incredulity at the lack of marketing targeted to blacks by mainstream corporations despite the overwhelming evidence that there are many viable African-American segments with a good deal of money to spend.

Kathryn Leary, a former vice president of Ted Bates Advertising in New York, and now president of Kathryn Leary Communications, says, "To not utilize the available marketing tools to analyze the nearly $300 billion African-American consumer market is to blatantly ignore the most basic marketing principles. Even cat lovers are carefully segmented and analyzed, with great concern for maximizing profit with the right advertising strategy. How does one miss this opportunity with the entire African-American population? It defies logic, and it defies marketing theory."

West Indian Blacks

In the early 1900s blacks from the rural South began to settle in northern industrial cities. They were joined by a new group—black immigrants from the Caribbean. By the 1920s a quarter of Harlem's population consisted of West Indians from Jamaica, Barbados, Trinidad, and other British West Indian islands. Interestingly, intermarriage rates for West Indians and American-born blacks have been very low, even when they live in the same communities and go to the same colleges.

Many descendants of the early West Indians immigrants have become successful professionals, business executives, and politicians. In the 1980s, however, poorer and less educated Caribbean blacks immigrated to the United States in search of economic opportunity; 214,000 Jamaicans, or 9 percent of the island's population, came to the United States. Large numbers have also come from Haiti and Guyana and from smaller countries such as Grenada and St. Kitts. New York, Miami, and other East Coast cities still receive many Caribbean immigrants, both legal and undocumented.

Some of these immigrants exhibit consumer behavior patterns that resemble those of other recent immigrant groups, such as Hispanics and Asians, more than those of U.S.-born blacks. For example, Haitians often mistrust banks and pool their money in informal credit unions known as *sou-sou*, much as Korean and Dominican immigrants utilize community-based forms of banking.

Haitians, in part because they're not native speakers of English, tend not to assimilate to the African-Americans who often live next door. Because, in their homeland, Haitians view American products as very desirable but expensive, they, and some other recent island immigrants, love finally accessible all-American treats such as Ritz crackers and Jell-O.

Cultural Values

When marketing to African-Americans, keep in mind that they value self-image, style, and personal elegance. Roland L. Freeman, author of *Philadelphia's African-Americans: A Celebration of Life*, writes, "Style—whether captured in an elegant hat, an eloquent phrase, a sophisticated step, or a smooth move—lies at the very heart of African-American culture."

African-Americans are trendsetters. Black culture has had a major impact on clothing, language, music, and dance, which has not only dominated U.S. youth culture but the entire global youthmarket. Trends begin in the inner cities of the United States, spread among mainstream American teens, and go on to influence teens around the world.

African-Americans often want to define their own style rather than follow what the establishment dictates. This may represent a desire to make the mainstream take notice of the black community or to encourage members of the black community to take notice of themselves. Whatever the reason, there is a strong desire, especially on the part of young blacks, to be recognized.

In past generations, African-Americans who sought recognition sometimes emulated the white upper class through conspicuous consumption of goods usually associated with wealth. (This same behavior was often seen in the immigrants who came to this country in the early 1900s. Lacking respect from the establishment and barred from living and socializing in better neighborhoods even if they could afford it, these immigrants bought the only symbols of wealth and success that were open to them: a Cadillac, premium whiskies, and expensive clothing.)

The advertising executive Eugene Morris says that many lower-income blacks buy expensive liquor to make a statement about themselves, because premium liquor is an affordable status symbol. Many inner-city youths wear an enormous amount of gold jewelry to convey status; gold, although fairly expensive, is more affordable and accessible than moving to a ritzy suburban house. Lower-income segments of the African-American market are innovators, too. They try trendy, new products, especially if they convey status or prestige. Middle-class and upper-class African-Americans also spend a large percentage of their incomes on luxury goods, such as new cars, fashionable clothing, and high-tech audio equipment, just as many segments of the general market do.

Felix Burrows, president of Viewpoint, Inc., of Chicago, believes that many middle-class blacks seek lifestyles that combine black culture and traditions with their increasing prosperity. "This market segment consists of consumers who aren't very interested in impressing whites and who prefer to interact mostly with their peers. They are independent and self-confident. Their selection of products and services reflects this lifestyle, which is quite different from that of whites."

Cultural Identity

A major issue for many middle- and upper-class blacks is the struggle between assimilation and Afrocentrism. Being both black and middle-class becomes a double bind when class and race are defined in sharply conflicting terms so that one side must be repressed to appease the other.

Listen to Chuck Morrison: "There are different subsegments in the African-American segment. Some people subscribe to the idea that if we prosper, we will lose our African-American identity. Can't. Can't rub this [color] off."

Professor Henry Louis Gates, Jr., says, "When I left for Yale, virtually my whole hometown celebrated. . . . Talking black, walking black, wearing Kente cloth, listening to black music, and filling our walls with black art—as desirable as these things can be in and of themselves—are not essential to being black. You can love Mozart, Picasso, and ice hockey and still be as black as the ace of spades."

Family and Religious Values

The sociologist Mitchell Duneier studied a group of older working-class black men on Chicago's South Side who met regularly at a cafeteria. His book, *Slim's Table*, records the sad observations of these men regarding the deteriorating quality of life in the ghettos and the decline in the values of the younger generation. The men are upset at the characterization of black men as lazy and repelled by the snobby "buppies" (black upwardly mobile professionals) who park their Mercedeses near the cafeteria on their way to nearby upscale restaurants.

All these men have high regard for respect and morality, and many hold conservative social and economic views like those of the "Reagan Democrats." Slim talks about the work ethic and the discipline of the past: "In our generation parents did what they called hands-on raising; your mother and father put their hand to you."

Family and religious values are very important to most African-Americans. More than six million people have attended the black weekend "festivals"—made up of many family reunions—begun in 1986 by the National Council of Negro Women. Dr. Dorothy I. Height, president of the council, said

in *The New York Times*: "We've had some six million in attendance in the last six years and not a single police incident. We
started these weekends in response to the negative projection
of the vanishing black family, and we plan the family reunions
within the festivals."

The marketing implications of feeding, sheltering, and
entertaining participants at black family reunions, which are
increasing in popularity, are phenomenal. Marc Michaelson,
spokesman for Motel 6, says that, once the company realized
the opportunity, "for the last two summers [1991 and 1992] 20
percent of our advertising budget has been targeted at family
reunions."

African-Americans are doing more group traveling and
convening than ever before. Many blacks prefer vacationing or
traveling with a group rather than on their own, which often
leaves them feeling isolated or worse. Affinity groups, from
associations of black skiers to groups of African-American
teachers and professors to political and cultural organizations,
are big business.

Thousands of black groups have money to spend on comfortable, stylish accommodations, music, entertainment and
good food. The providers of goods and service who go out of
their way to accommodate the preferences, needs, and interests
of these groups will find a loyal market of mid- and upscale
consumers.

Religion and church are also very important to many
African-Americans. For many, the ritual of traditional Christianity blended with the call-and-response gospel rhythms
rooted in African heritage provides a comforting identity. An
estimated 5 million who feel better represented by their African
heritage celebrate Kwaanza instead of or in addition to Christmas; from December 26 to January 1, they eat African foods
and celebrate African culture. Others have chosen Islam, and
in many urban centers African-American Moslems attend services at mosques and follow the teachings of Mohammed.

Marketers who reach out to church groups with sensitivity
and respect can effectively reach a powerful and influential
segment within the black community. McDonald's sponsors
the Gospel Explosion on the Black Entertainment Television

(BET) network; Quaker Oats funded free health screening clinics in black churches during Black History Month and donated blood-pressure machines for the churches' year-round health programs.

On a smaller scale, some savvy marketers, individually or together, distribute complimentary samples of their brands at church services or festivals. As with the Asian and Hispanic markets, it's a good deal more effective to show a corporate commitment to the black community on a year-round basis than to offer a one-shot push.

Black-Owned Business

Along with spending on travel and entertainment, African-Americans are in the business of business. Wells Fargo Bank, United Health Plan, Shell Oil, the *Los Angeles Sentinel* newspaper, and other companies sponsored the Fifth Annual Los Angeles Black Business Expo in 1993 to allow vendors and providers to network with prospective buyers. Forums of this type attract entrepreneurs and corporations of all sizes and provide an opportunity for companies to show their commitment to minority businesses.

Market Research Issues

Because the African-American market is as diverse as the mainstream market, those interested in selling to it must research, segment, and target with relevance. Dr. David Stewart, professor of marketing at the University of Southern California, believes that there's a fine line between trying to appeal to taste and ethnic heritage and creating a stereotype.

Marketers need to target the African-American market without fostering stereotypes, offending sensibilities, or lumping segments together. First, do research. When designing questionnaires, adapt issues so they are culturally relevant to the market and its segments. Surveys must be undertaken from the customer's perspective. And we need to design separate, relevant research questions for each subsegment.

Market research techniques need to be restructured; few techniques used for the general market are appropriate for the black consumer or for other ethnic and minority markets. Especially in urban areas, for example, few people bother to fill out the data information cards that accompany appliances and other purchases. The majority of the research information gathered from these cards comes from suburban and often upscale consumers, giving a skewed picture of consumer preferences and buying behavior that eliminates the black perspective.

Second, we must bring in people who are experienced with and knowledgeable about the segments we are targeting at the outset of the marketing campaign. In the ethnic market, that means more than tokenism—but it shouldn't exclude trained and sensitive marketers who are not African-Americans. Many nonblack women marketers, having struggled against discrimination in the marketplace and elsewhere in their lives, can be highly empathic toward African-Americans. Although there are certainly many sensitive white males in the industry, research shows that women usually take more time to learn about the customer's needs, interests, preferences and lifestyle without becoming impatient or seeming patronizing.

After doing research—with the segmentation studies that are already available and with more, better interpreted, accurate, and measurable information—we need to coordinate campaigns with market-savvy consultants and agencies. Then we can design advertising and promotional campaigns that accurately reflect the market. Of course, it's expensive, but the payback is always a higher return on the investment than with the general market.

Targeted Products

Savvy marketers around the country are beginning to wake up to the opportunity presented by products specifically designed for African-Americans. In 1980 it was almost impossible to get makeup formulated for darker skins; now practically every major cosmetics company has jumped on the bandwagon. A recent offering is Ebone, a new line from the black-owned Johnson Publishing Company (which, in addition to its highly successful magazines, *Ebony* and *Jet*, had an earlier line of cosmetics for older women, called Fashion Fair). The company looks forward to great response to the less pricey new line for young women, which is advertised in *Ebony* and *Jet*.

Many people feel that cosmetics from a black-owned company have an advantage over the mainstream giants, which have long been associated with ads featuring blue-eyed blondes. (In a recent survey of magazine ads, Cover Girl showed only one minority model out of 236 ads.)

There are other great opportunities that could only have come from a true understanding of African-American consumer needs. *Essence* magazine, in a licensing arrangement, created a line of designer eyewear for people with broad features. The glasses have a broader nose bridge and longer temple stems, which differentiate them from other eyeglasses. This unique construction is comfortable for African-Americans and is highly stylish.

A fair number of black men wear beards because of the problems they have during shaving. Black facial hair curls back after being shaved, creating bumps that can scar after repeated cuts. Edgar Morris Mitchell, a Los Angeles skin-care specialist, has created a kit containing a special beard softener and other skin-care products formulated for black men's skin.

Other opportunities are just beginning to be capitalized upon. An African-American woman colleague of mine complained that manufacturers of women's clothing never take into account the physical differences between black and white women. Research has shown that some African-American women are steatopygic (have higher and rounder buttocks). Because most women's clothing is designed for the buttocks of white women, skirts and dresses tend to bunch up or ride up uncomfortably on black women. In 1993, a joint venture of Spiegel, Inc., and *Ebony* magazine came out with E Style, a 64-page catalog offering well-cut clothing for African-American women.

Some retailers are beginning to cater to African-American

tastes and needs. Speaking in *Marketing News* about J.C. Penney's successful Authentic African boutiques, Bruce Ackerman, the chain's merchandising operations manager, says, "Minority supplier development isn't a social thing anymore. It's bringing to the consumer what the consumer wants."

Afrocentric boutiques and stores offer a wide range of African clothing and fabrics for the home. Many are based on Kente cloth, which is a variety of richly patterned fabric produced in West Africa. It was originally worn by African royalty to signify power, prestige, and style and is woven of cotton and, sometimes, silk. Kente cloth was traditionally worn by men as a toga and by women as a dress. In America, it signifies black pride, and many blacks say that Kente cloth helps them appreciate the African in African-American.

And it's not just clothing that's in demand. At Prince George's Plaza in Prince George's County, Maryland, near Washington, D.C., the upscale customers who live in the area can choose among national chain stores and several smaller shops. Pyramid Books stocks its shelves with a wide range of titles dealing with African and African-American issues. Pyramid carries books and publications not routinely stocked in a general market store and advertises in such publications as the *Washington Afro-American & Tribune*, the *Baltimore Afro-American*, the student newspaper at Howard University, and by direct mail.

In the last few years, sales of ethnic foods have exploded. Supermarkets regularly stock products catering to different ethnic tastes and do great business with both targeted ethnic groups and the crossover market of mainstream consumers who want ethnic foods. Only in recent years, however, has prepared food been specifically developed and targeted to the African-American market. Glory Foods, an Ohio-based minority-owned company, test-marketed a line of packaged soul food. Its cornbread mix, collard greens, okra, and other items were a great hit in the ninety test-market stores, and a national rollout began in 1993.

Judging by how mainstream consumers have gobbled up (literally) ethnic foods from Afghan to Vietnamese over the past few years, it's a sure bet that they will quickly take to packaged soul food as well. Wiley Mullins, whose Uncle Wiley's canned vegetables are selling well on the affluent upper East Side of Manhattan, reports that some of his strongest markets are in nonblack areas populated by younger, well-educated whites.

For years, black children had little choice but to play with white dolls, read comics geared to a white audience, and listen to fairy tales about Goldilocks. Today, there are products that African-American children can enjoy and identify with. Huggy Bean dolls, from Golden Ribbon Playthings in New York, are not just white dolls with black faces but actually look like children of African descent. The company also publishes African adventure books and manufactures Kulture Kids, smaller dolls wearing Kente clothes.

Milestone Media has an agreement with DC Comics, Inc., in New York to produce a line of comic books featuring blacks as heroes. Derek T. Dingle, president of Milestone, loved comics as a child, but he never saw any heroes in them that looked like him—none were African-American. So Mr. Dingle will produce a line of comic books that will feature not only blacks but women, Hispanics, and Asians.

Inter Image Video, a company that specializes in African and African-American entertainment and educational videos for adults and children, offers "Dreadlocks and the Three Bears," which reinvents the children's fairy tale to teach lessons about self-esteem and living in peace with others.

The Black Gold National Shoppers Guide, published by Communications Problem Solvers of Chicago, lists more than 1,000 black designers, sculptors, painters, merchants, and distributors and is a clearinghouse for goods and services offered by black artists and merchants. It is available in some national book chains.

Investing in Black America

Most of the Afrocentric products that have been received with great enthusiasm have been designed and marketed by blacks. Many of the small businesses that produce these products, however, have long and unhappy histories related to their efforts to obtain financing to start up their operations, expand them, or change direction. Like women and immigrants, blacks have faced tremendous discrimination in lending.

The chief operating officer of Rebuild Los Angeles, Bernard W. Kinsey, a former executive at Xerox and himself black, said, in *The New York Times*, "When I hear someone say they're not investing in a business or a person or an idea because it's in the inner city or because it involves a person of color, I say you're not assessing your risk the right way or in the way you do in other situations. Bankers always say it's a high-risk area, but these are the people who lent to Latin America and bought junk bonds and financed every half-empty high-rise tower in the country."

It's not only black entrepreneurs who have trouble building a business. Mainstream companies that want to serve black communities sometimes have trouble getting financing. And some retailers avoid black neighborhoods, even if they aren't low-income areas; some leave inner-city neighborhoods when they become predominately black. In Boston, thirty-four of the fifty big-chain supermarkets have closed their stores since 1970. In Los Angeles County, only 695 supermarkets are left from the more than 1,000 that existed in 1970.

The South DeKalb Mall, which became such a hit in an Atlanta suburb, attracted Jeans West and the Avenue but lost a Florsheim Shoe Shop and a B. Dalton bookstore. And the mall says that it went after four national chains in one year, only to encounter resistance. What's puzzling is that more than 40 percent of the households in the mall's zip code earn more than $50,000 a year.

But there are good signs, too. In 1990 Newark's New Community Corporation persuaded Supermarkets General to open a Pathmark supermarket in the city's central ward—the first new chain market there since 1976. The store has become a good business venture with seemingly few problems.

The British entrepreneur Anita Roddick's Body Shop opened an outlet in Harlem in 1992, the only one of her 118 stores not operating as a franchise. (This New Age toiletries chain began with one small shop in England and became the rage in the United States when branches opened in high-traffic areas such as malls and upscale shopping centers.) The Harlem Body Shop, with its environmentally conscious products, does no animal testing and asks customers to bring in their lotion containers to be refilled. The store is a loss leader, intended to lure other upscale outlets to the neighborhood. At least half of its profits are pledged to charities, and its employees are exclusively black and Hispanic.

Just across the street from the Body Shop in Harlem is a Ben & Jerry's ice cream shop, the fourth in a social program founded by Ben & Jerry's in 1987 in which the usual franchise fee of $25,000 is waived. Joseph Holland, a black, Harvard-trained lawyer, decided to become an entrepreneur in the black community. Mr. Holland, who owns the Harlem shop, pledged 60 percent of its net proceeds to a men's shelter in the neighborhood.

And under the stewardship of Bernard Kinsey, Rebuild Los Angeles has gotten major corporate contributions and investment pledges—from Vons Companies to build inner-city supermarkets, from Hughes Aircraft Company to contract with minority suppliers, from Mattel to establish four Mattel Learning Centers for inner-city children, from Pioneer Electronics to finance job-training programs for the electronics industry, from Nissan Motor Corporation, USA, to establish an endowment fund for economic development, from Southern California Edison to donate money and services for job-training centers, and from the New York Life Insurance Company to help finance community improvement programs.

These companies know that their futures depend not only on the mainstream consumers of America but on the ethnics and the minorities who will soon make up the majority of California's population. Smart companies like these are investing in their own futures by showing consumers that they want to make things better in the consumers' communities. And it's smart advertising, too. The goodwill that the publicity generates for these companies is far greater than anything that could be achieved by ads in the print or the electronic media.

No one can deny the tremendous changes that have occurred since the we-shall-overcome years of struggle of the

1960s, fueled by the hope that the civil rights movement put into the hearts of many, both black and white. But it seems that economics may have a more powerful effect on racial issues in the 1990s. Let's go one step further and realize that now is the time for mainstream marketers to practice inclusion, rather than exclusion. Here's the opportunity for companies to enter into a win-win relationship—satisfying the consumer needs of African-Americans while earning higher corporate profits.

An Interview With Debra Sandler, Pepsico, Inc.

In this interview, Debra Sandler, Director of Flavor Brands for Pepsico, offers valuable insights into Pepsi's continued success in the African-American market.

Q: Please give a little background information on yourself.

DS: I am Marketing Director for Flavor Brands at Pepsi. That includes every carbonated soft drink that we sell that is not cola. That includes Mountain Dew, Slice, Mug root beer, and Mug creme soda, and some frozen carbonated products. We also have some products in test, for example, Mirinda, which is a Hispanic flavor line, and there are a few other things that we are looking at. Basically, the group totals about $3 billion in annual sales.

I've been at Pepsi seven years, with a number of assignments. Prior to my current position, I was director of ethnic consumer marketing.

Q: How did ethnic marketing evolve at Pepsico? And how have you been involved in the evolution of the ethnic marketing programs?

DS: We've been at this for quite some time. Our efforts can be traced back to the early 1940s, when hiring practices included ethnic recruiting. I am happy to say that we were progressive not only from an ethnic standpoint but also from a gender standpoint, hiring both male and female sales people to sell to the African-American community.

These people were also commission-based. So we've been at this in various forms for quite some time.

I would say that most companies go through a very clear and specific evolution as they begin to get involved in segment marketing. One way is that they typically start off with public relations activities, sponsorships, local dinners and events, and so forth. Then it progresses to a specific promotion or one or two promotions a year to get to this particular consumer. If the company is progressive enough, it will evolve to where I believe we are now and that is applying the fully marketing discipline to the target market.

So you're not just looking at sponsorships and promotions, you're looking at a strategic plan, a comprehensive program including packaging, pricing, a media plan, and the product offering. As companies get involved, I think it's a pretty clear evolution along that path.

Q: *What kind of research do you use?*

DS: We do consumer tracking several times a year where we talk to consumers about what they think of our products, how it relates to their lifestyle, what they think of our advertising and promotion, and so forth. It is ongoing. In addition to that, we do proprietary research to get a clearer sense of any particular issue.

For example, on a given brand, we got feedback from consumers that they didn't think the brand was relevant to their lifestyle. We did some additional research to understand why the brand wasn't relevant. Was it the advertising, the brand, the packaging? Specifically, what was driving the perception?

We found out that it was perception driven by our copy in our advertising. This was on a significantly smaller brand than Pepsi. We addressed the problem by changing some of the copy and by going a step further and changing a few other things to make sure that we are relevant.

Quite honestly, one of the best things is feedback from our front line—our sales force—the people who are dealing with customers and consumers on a day-to-day basis. At Pepsi, employee feedback is some of the very best.

Q: *Comment on your management and how it views ethnic target marketing. Are they aware of the return on profit opportunities? How does the company allocate money to ethnic marketing programs?*

DS: We no longer speak of ethnic marketing efforts in social-responsibility, corporate-responsibility, or "feel-good" terms. Rather, we speak in terms of the case opportunity, the profit opportunity, how much we've got in market share, and how much we think we can get if we invest.

Q: *Can you discuss in detail how the elements, from product development to advertising and promotion, differ for the African-American target market?*

DS: If you think about what we sell, it could easily be considered a commodity-type product. We don't have a specific soda or brand that is designed and marketed purely to the African-American consumer. What we do have are brands that are preferred by African-American consumers. So what we try to do is to make sure that we are meeting the needs of those consumers.

For example, we know through research that African-Americans prefer regular colas to diet colas. Whether that is a function of habit or whether that is something we have created ourselves doesn't really matter. The fact is, the numbers today say that African-Americans are drinking more regular colas than diet colas, and they are drinking a disproportionate amount of flavored soft drinks other than colas, like Slice and Mountain Dew. Consequently, we use this information to ensure that our message reaches and is relevant to these consumers.

Q: *How does the strategy differ for African-American marketing in comparison to the mainstream marketing strategy?*

DS: The strategy does not differ, the tactics differ. For example, if we say we want to be the beverage of choice to all teens, one of the things we have to do if we want to get to where teens are, to where they live and breathe, is to be wherever they are. We want to be available; we also want to be seen as part of their lifestyle. The difference is that we may go about that differently for an eighteen-year-old Anglo male who lives in the suburbs than for an eighteen-year-old African-American male who happens to live in an urban environment.

For example, we did a promotion where we gave away prizes—jet skis and convertibles. One thing we heard loud and clear from the urban teens was that they didn't participate in the promotion because they didn't think the prizes were relevant. So sometimes the tactics must change. But unless there are some reasons why the strategy will not work, the strategy won't vary. While we, African-American consumers, are our own segment, we are also very much a part of the mainstream. In fact, in many cases we are driving the mainstream.

So to say that you are going to target only this particular group actually obscures the dividing line, especially in contrast to thirty or forty years ago. Again, in reaching teens, if I can produce television creative that appeals to an urban eighteen-year-old male, chances are that creative will appeal to all teens. It doesn't always work the other way around.

Q: *Can you comment about the cultural differences that may be overlooked by mainstream companies in the development of an ethnic marketing strategy?*

DS: Clearly, there are differences in multicultural marketing. We'll use as an example the strategy to make Pepsi the brand of choice for teens ages twelve to eighteen. That strategy is not going to change for African-Americans twelve to eighteen. What does change is the way we enact that strategy. That is where the cultural differences come into play.

It's funny because I was an international business major in my undergraduate studies, and I often feel like I am doing international marketing in the domestic environment. Yes, you must take into account the cultural differences. That, in my mind, is how you bring your strategy to life for that consumer.

Q: *What are some of the opportunities for your company in this area? Is it growing more into lifestyle marketing for ethnic targeted segments?*

DS: I think we have an opportunity to continue to learn more. I think lifestyle marketing is one area that we will experiment with. I get a little nervous when we start talking about products that are targeted specifically for this consumer. There are companies that have tried that before and have failed miserably.

Q: *What do you believe are the opportunities in general for companies targeting ethnic market segments? Are there untapped opportunities in this particular market segment, and has Pepsi pursued them?*

DS: There are still a lot. One of the challenges I think is how to get this done on a regional level where we have local application and local relevance, while taking advantage of national efficiencies—in other words, taking what we learn from Detroit and applying it to Atlanta. How to combine national and regional focus to make it one effort? That's a major challenge. There is a school of thought that says that ethnic target marketing can be done only on a regional level.

But there are many people who feel that there are national synergies that need to be developed. Your overall strategy should be national, but your execution should be regional. Actually, we could go back and forth on that one for a long time. That is an ongoing challenge as we continue to decentralize our organization. Where and how do you centralize this effort, if at all? That's one of the things for us to figure out.

Q: Could you discuss the challenges in execution?

DS: OK. Let's talk about a company that compensates its front line on commissions. So, for example, let's say that Pepsi's front line is being compensated on a commission basis. Well, it could be argued that what we are thereby doing is encouraging our front-line people to hit the large suburban stores where the store can take hundreds of cases of soft drinks, storing them either on the floors or in the back room.

That person, putting in one hour's worth of work, can drop off many more cases than the salesperson who is calling on the inner-city stores, where the stores are smaller—they don't have back rooms, they are not going to take more than twenty to twenty-five cases. This is a very real execution issue. It is not an issue tied to targeting an African-American consumer—an ethnic consumer issue. But it has tremendous impact because it is often the ethnic consumer shopping in those inner-city stores.

For example, when it comes to promotion activities, like Black History Month, is it better for us to spend at headquarters to develop one promotion that we execute throughout the country, or do we give the top five or ten markets the budget and allow them to spend against local needs? That's the national-versus-regional argument. What is the best way to spend your money? The answer is, What do you really want to achieve? Those are the kinds of things that we are thinking through and that many companies must begin to address.

Q: Is there anything else you would like to add?

DS: We have found that success is a three-pronged effort. The first piece is credibility with the consumer or marketplace. That credibility can be derived—and that is one of the things that public relations does so well. They get us involved in the community, get us seen in the events that are important to the community. That communicates to people in the community that you care and makes you a credible voice. Credibility is critical, and public relations plays a strong role there. Also workforce diversity plays a role there. So credibility is the first thing.

The second thing is relevance—taking into account everything. We are, some say, a marketing-driven company. So it's important to take a look at all the elements of the marketing mix to address the issue of relevance. For example, when we do a promotion, if we know that African-American consumers prefer two-liter packages over twenty-four-can packages, we probably don't want to do a promotion with twenty-four cans. Relevance—take everything into account—product, price, promotion, place. Apply the marketing discipline, and think about relevance.

The final thing is ubiquity. Make sure that your execution is perfect—that you are everywhere the consumer is. And for a product like ours, it's important that whenever a consumer gets the notion, we are there. These are the things, these three things, that in tandem are critical.

Q: *How would you say your copy differs from that of Coca-Cola?*

DS: I think we've been more inclusive. Interestingly enough, the inclusion has been many African-American protagonists—Bo Jackson, Young MC, Ray Charles, Shaquille O'Neal. We had them as protagonists largely because they were leading-edge, they were interesting, entertaining, fun. And for this particular target group, African-Americans, our advertising recognizes and acknowledges them. Certainly, this has helped people to identify with the company.

7

Diverse America: Some Other Segments

It's been encouraging to see that print and television ads no longer exclusively feature young, perfectly gorgeous, toothy, blonde, blue-eyed models. We've begun to see plain-looking people, people of color, adults and children with disabilities, seniors, and men with receding hairlines. For most of us, seeing more real-world types is not only a relief from unrelenting, unrealistic perfection but also a chance to see people we can identify with. They represent America today.

Ads in mail-order fashion catalogs have featured an attractive woman wearing leg braces, a fifty-plus "silver fox," a handsome man with an artificial leg, an adorable child in a wheelchair, and a happy-looking child with Down Syndrome. The consuming public is increasingly made up of these and many other segments, far too many for a lengthy discussion in this book.

Some of these segments, although very large in number, can't be defined by ethnicity or national origin, yet are to some degree or other separate from the mainstream. These groups include senior citizens, homosexuals, and people with physical or mental disabilities.

The important thing is to learn about these segments—how to reach them and how to design an appropriate marketing strategy. In many cases, all that's necessary is to reach out to the group by advertising or promoting in group-specific or regional media. In other cases, sincere, long-term commitment to a promotional strategy, rather than tokenism, in ads featuring members of the target group is needed.

Native Americans

One group that is usually overlooked are the nearly 2 million Native Americans, or American Indians. There are many tribes, of which the largest are the Cherokee, with more than 300,000 members, the Navajo, with more than 200,000, and the Chippewa and the Sioux, with more than 100,000 each. There are hundreds of other tribes, most with fewer than 1,000 members each.

Native Americans were the first inhabitants of North and South America, having crossed over from Asia between 25,000 and 50,000 years ago. These people of color were called Indians by Christopher Columbus, who thought he was in Asia when he had in fact landed in the Dominican Republic. The different tribes speak many different languages, but their rich cultures share many characteristics, including a reverence for nature.

The Europeans who came to the Americas after Columbus are frequently accused of exploiting the Native Americans throughout North and South America. However, over the years, many American Indians have intermarried with whites and blacks. It's always refreshing when someone proudly says that they're one-eighth Indian or they had an Indian grandparent.

Today, most Native Americans live in the western United States, especially in Kansas, Nebraska, North Dakota, South Dakota, Montana, Arizona, New Mexico, and Washington. There are also many Indians in Minnesota, Wisconsin, Michigan, and California, and some smaller groups live in some eastern states.

Persistent poverty has been an ongoing problem for American Indians. Unemployment rates are as high as 80 percent. To counter poor educational conditions on Indian reservations, Native Americans are turning to tribal colleges for learning opportunities and for cultural values. More than 13,000 students are now enrolled in these twenty-six colleges, twenty-four of them on reservations. One way to reach out to Native Americans is to support these colleges, which constitute the perfect opportunity to show interest in this almost totally ignored segment.

In the last few years, mainstream America has demonstrated a growing interest in Native American culture. This interest has been reflected in a number of Hollywood movies about Indians, including *Thunderheart, Dances with Wolves,* and *Last of the Mohicans.* Major companies are selling sneakers, T-shirts, caps, and sweatshirts decorated with Native American beads and designed by Indians. Reebok, an especially astute marketer, has contributed to the Native American Arts Foundation, which helps Indians market their crafts.

Clothing, arts and crafts, and toys made by Native Americans or depicting their lifestyle have become big sellers. But when designing a promotional strategy, don't fall into the trap of the feather-and-tomahawk stereotype. Taking the time to learn about the needs and interests of today's Native Americans will earn a loyal following.

Americans With Disabilities

An estimated 43 million Americans have disabilities. Some have severe disabilities and must use wheelchairs, others have impairments that are not immediately visible, such as arthritis, deafness, and some forms of mental retardation. Americans with disabilities cut across the entire demographic spectrum. Some were born with their disability, some have become disabled through illness or accident.

Whatever the reason, disabled people, once relegated to a life of dependency behind closed doors, are becoming more independent and are living satisfying lives. The Americans With Disabilities Act, which went into effect in 1992, ensures that employers would provide access and facilities for disabled workers and bans discrimination against the more than 14 million disabled working-age Americans. The law also requires public facilities to be accessible to all, even if it means, among other things, providing braille or large-type menus for blind people; installing wheelchair-accessible windows and automatic teller machines at banks; providing ramps and space for wheelchairs at theaters; making restrooms accessible to the disabled, and designing wide aisles in supermarkets that can accommodate wheelchairs.

Although the law went into effect in 1992, it will take a long time before all the businesses covered reach full compliance, for it is costly to retrofit businesses, transportation, and recreational facilities. In the meantime, many companies are not only hiring talented workers with disabilities but are going out of their way to come up with products and services that meet their needs. Most workers with disabilities earn less than mainstream workers, but they spend plenty of money on the products that make their lives easier.

Over 7 million disabled Americans live in homes that have been adapted to accommodate their special need. Some disabled individuals live in traditional families; others live with special caregivers and other disabled people in group facilities. Taking the families and caregivers into consideration when selling goods and services to the disabled, there clearly is a huge market of potential consumers.

By showing ads with disabled actors, companies are recognizing that the disabled are a real and viable part of American life. McDonald's, AT&T, Apple Computer, Budweiser, Citibank, Pacific Bell, Olympus, and Kmart seem to be saying that their offerings are worthy, and so are people with disabilities. What ad could be more of a winner than a cute kid in a wheelchair going to McDonald's for a burger and fries?

And while mainstream ads may show only a brief shot of a person in a wheelchair or include only one disabled model among a group of able-bodied people, such ads nonetheless send powerful messages of inclusion to this huge group, which buys soda and breakfast cereals, beer and socks—the same things that everyone buys. But seeing a disabled person in a company's ad sets their products apart from the competition.

These marketing campaigns are undertaken not just to demonstrate social responsibility but to win loyal customers and market share. For example, Citibank took the hokey, feel-good kind of lost credit card ad that we can all identify with a step further. Its ad showed a deaf woman getting her lost Visa card replaced by signing on a telecommunications device for the deaf, combining a common customer service with new technology.

There are many products that are specifically designed for the disabled—from voice-activated computer software for people who can't use their hands, to a device that turns computer text into audible speech, to an aid that makes it easier for disabled hands to type. IBM, Digital Equipment, Apple, and Hewlett-Packard are among the forward-thinking companies offering these and other innovations that make everyone's life easier and better.

And it's not just big companies that are producing these enablers. *Managing Information Resources for Accessibility*, a resource guide put out by the U.S. General Services Administration, lists products manufactured by companies of all sizes. A mail-order catalog put out by AdaptAbility of Colchester, Connecticut, includes forty-four pages of products to make the lives of the disabled (and abled) much more comfortable. The ads for this catalog feature able-bodied and disabled people, seniors, and people of color.

As with African-Americans, companies traditionally stayed away from ads featuring the disabled because they feared alienating their mainstream customers. But according to Bob Thacker, marketing vice president of Target Stores, speaking in *Marketing News*, "Items modeled by people with disabilities have sold as well as or better than things modeled by able-bodied individuals."

Old stereotypes are being shattered constantly. Consider the Budweiser ad that shows a wheelchair-bound male athlete with his nondisabled girlfriend, talking about celebrating his victory by enjoying sex. The acclaimed television show "Life Goes On," featuring a young retarded man living in the mainstream, has gone a long way toward educating the public about retardation and Down Syndrome; the disabled character was played by Chris Burke, an actor who has Down Syndrome.

For children with Down Syndrome, there is Dolly Downs, a pigtailed doll with the broad face and angled eyes that characterize this form of retardation. Dolly Downs is assembled by retarded and developmentally disabled workers at Camp Venture Inc., in Stony Point, New York. She comes with a storybook and a tape, and her character is an advocate of community group homes for the retarded.

In New York and in other large cities, shops that sell products for the deaf have been flourishing. Sign of the Times Bookstore sells, among other items to make life easier for the deaf, an alarm clock that is tucked under the pillow and shakes the person awake. Travel programs for the disabled, who very much want to have fun, are booming.

The 75 or so million baby boomers are aging and will become increasingly vulnerable to age-related disabilities such as arthritis and impaired vision. With the boomers' clout, a new movement—"universal design"—will appeal to a mass market. The movement's aim is to make products that can be used by disabled individuals but that are also easy for everyone to use—kitchen utensils with big handles, phones with large buttons, tubs with doors, and easy-open boxes and containers.

Gays and Lesbians

Although estimates vary wildly, the U.S. homosexual population is probably somewhere between 5 and 20 million, although not nearly that many are openly gay. Only a relatively small fraction of homosexual Americans are "out" and are active gay consumers.

In the early 1990s, after decades of ignoring affluent homosexuals, mainstream companies began targeting this market by advertising in gay and lesbian magazines. Companies like Philip Morris, Absolut Vodka, Virgin Atlantic Airways, Time Warner, and Hiram Walker are just a few of the companies that began taking advantage of this large and often brand-loyal segment. One reason for their action may be that in a recessionary economy, companies quickly become liberal and nonjudgmental. Most of the companies that target gays agree that they're not making a political statement, just employing an advertising strategy.

However, many companies have yet to acknowledge the

existence of the gay market, expecting to reach it through the mainstream media. Although most homosexual men and women are reached through mainstream media, the gay media are also growing. Gays want to see products and services targeted to them through gay magazines and newspapers and through sponsorships.

The average household income for gay men is about $52,000 and for lesbians, almost $43,000, according to Overlooked Opinions, of Chicago, a market research firm, because many gays are "dinks," the psychographic term for that desirable state of being a household with *double income, no kids*. With two or fewer persons per household, and with more than 40 percent having household incomes in excess of $60,000, gays are a dream market.

The total estimate of gay income is somewhere around $500 billion. Were they white and heterosexual, gays would be targeted by purveyors of every good and service imaginable. Many gays and lesbians are highly educated and hold managerial and professional jobs. They cluster primarily in urban areas like New York, San Francisco, Los Angeles, Chicago, and Miami, but they live everywhere in America. They also tend to favor expensive suburbs and areas around major university centers. Dave Mulryan, director of business development at Mulryan/Nash Communications, a New York ad agency specializing in the gay market, says, "Gay spending power is about urban, highly educated populations that are easy to segment and target by zip codes."

Gays are avid consumers of luxury goods and services and spend a good deal on restaurants, fine wines, state-of-the-art stereo and electronic equipment, books, travel, clothing, and entertainment. Gay men are well-respected trendsetters with plenty of discretionary income. Many don't have children and therefore don't have to pay for children's college tuition, clothing, books, bikes, and furnishings.

Gay men and lesbian women are especially good targets for certain industries. They are avid readers and travelers— good targets for book clubs and travel agencies. Strub Media Group in Rockland County, New York, sells mailing lists to book clubs and other mainstream companies from its database of more than 300,000 gay and lesbian names. Simmons Market Research Bureau in New York reports that more than 72 percent of gays take airplane trips, four times more than the national average. Gays travel 7.5 times the average to foreign destinations.

Many travel agencies, resorts, and hotels target gays by positioning themselves as gay-oriented or gay-friendly. Luxurious ocean cruises have become very popular; in this welcoming atmosphere, gays can relax without having to pretend or posture for the straight world. Olivia, in Oakland, California, a popular cruise company catering to lesbians, has attracted more than 4,500 passengers over a three-year period.

Many mainstream companies say that they don't target gays, not because of homophobia, but because of lack of data. Although many gays and lesbians have openly stated their sexual preference, a large number are still uncomfortable about identifying themselves as gay. Sarah Craig of Overlooked Opinions, speaking in *American Demographics* magazine, says, "It's an absence of documentation. That's one of the reasons we're in business. Marketers aren't going to respond until they have significant, reliable numbers."

But Dave Mulryan says, "We've had inquiries from a lot of companies. It's going to be a big thing, but have we had General Motors call? No, and it probably won't happen for a while."

The companies that have targeted gays have won a great many loyal consumers. Remy Martin, the only cognac to advertise in local gay media, has become the leading cognac in the gay community. This is another example of relevance. When gays see ads for the cognac in a gay newspaper, they feel that they not only are being acknowledged but are being respected as consumers. More than 85 percent of gays in a Simmons study said they would buy products or services that advertised in gay publications.

Over the past few years, there has been tremendous growth in gay-owned businesses, from greeting card companies to bicycle shops to bookstores and even including entire catalog companies selling gay-oriented products. Many gay and lesbian consumers would go out of their way to buy goods and services from other homosexuals. They say it's more comfortable to do business with gay business owners in their communities. Most gay and lesbian bookstores are owned by gays and lesbians themselves, and in a decade the number of such bookstores has grown from ten to more than fifty.

There's no shortage of gay media. Gays and lesbians can be targeted with more than 200 magazines and newspapers nationally. Some of the well-respected major publications include the *Bay Area Reporter* in San Francisco, the *New York Native*, *Frontiers* in Los Angeles, *The Dallas Voice*, the *Windy City Times* in Chicago, and *Bay Windows* in Boston.

The Advocate, the granddaddy of all gay media, circulates around 120,000 copies and had ad revenues of about $4.5 million in 1992. Another well-respected magazine is *Outweek*. *Outlook*, an intellectual and political magazine, sold more than 17,000 copies each quarter as early as 1990. The newest magazine, *Out* (which included an ad from Benetton—a first for the fashion industry), sold more than 10,000 subscriptions before it hit newsstands in June 1992.

Another good way to reach out to gays is through sponsorships and cause-related marketing. The fourth annual Gay Games (New York, 1994), is a prime opportunity for companies to capitalize on the gay consumer's spending power. Advertisers need to think of the event in the way that Nora Beverages, marketer of popular Naya spring water, does. Stewart Levitan, vice president of Nora, says that his company's decision to be the first company to sponsor the event was a marketing decision, not a lifestyle choice. Upscale consumers everywhere are drinking bottled water in ever-increasing amounts. And if gays and lesbians drink bottled water, it's probably going to be Naya, rather than the competition.

Although AIDS strikes heterosexuals as well as homosexuals, many gay communities have been devastated by the disease. An excellent way to win the purchasing loyalty of gays and lesbians (in fact, of almost everyone, gay and straight) is to join the growing list of companies that contribute to AIDS research and allied causes.

Companies can also reap the benefits of the consumer purchasing power of the gay community by having strong nondiscrimination policies, like those at Apple and Levi Strauss, which are among the few companies that specifically ban discrimination against gays. It's easy to guess that when gays buy computers and jeans, they buy Apple and Levi's.

Lotus was the first large, privately held company to give benefits to "domestic partners." By 1992, twenty-five cities, counties, and states, including New York City, San Francisco, Minneapolis, and the state of Washington, had established some form of legalized domestic partnership or had offered medical benefits or parental leave to partners of unmarried government workers.

Kosher and Halal

Religion can sometimes be used to segment a market. Although the number of Jews in the United States is stable at about 6 million, the percentage who are kosher (observe traditional religious rules on how animals are slaughtered and what foods can be eaten) is growing.

The kosher food market has been growing by 15 to 20 percent annually since 1980. There are more than 20,000 food products that are certified kosher, and thousands of mainstream companies, including Nestle, Hershey, Coca-Cola, Kraft, General Mills, and Coors, have obtained kosher certifications from one of the ninety-seven kosher-certifying organizations in the United States. The kosher certifications now appear on brands ranging from Snapple juices to Pez candy to Dannon yogurt.

Menachem Lubinsky of Integrated Marketing Communications, a kosher marketing consulting firm, estimates that U.S. sales of kosher-certified products totaled $35 billion in 1992, of which he estimates $2 billion represented sales to consumers who specifically seek out kosher products.

Some large mainstream food companies, including General Foods' Birds Eye vegetables, Post cereals, Maxwell House, Yuban, and Sanka coffees, and Domino sugar, regularly advertise in Jewish publications. Standard Brands, Tetley, Seagrams, Kelloggs, and others also target the kosher consumer.

Interestingly, a growing group of nonkosher Jews and Gentiles have showed increased interest in buying kosher meats and poultry because of the humane manner in which the animals are slaughtered and the freshness and cleanliness associated with kosher products.

"Health-conscious (nonkosher) consumers are definitely a growing part of our business," says Birgitta Wade, director of advertising of Empire Kosher Poultry, quoted in *The Wall Street Journal.* "Kosher is the Good Housekeeping Seal of the 1990s," agrees Joe Regenstein of the National Kosher Foods trade association.

Observant Jews are not the only religious group to require special foods. America has close to 4 million Moslems, including immigrants from the Middle East, Africa, and Asia and many black Americans who have adopted Islam. Observant Moslems eat "halal" food, which is similar in some ways to kosher; for example, no pork is eaten. In both kosher and halal observance, adherents are forbidden to eat any products from pigs, which are considered unclean. Moslems frequently buy kosher meat and chicken because they conform to the requirements of halal. Seventh-Day Adventists also seek out kosher food.

Many products, such as fresh vegetables and grains, are automatically kosher and halal unless they are processed with lard or other animal products. Only a relatively small expense for supervision is necessary to have these products certified by one of the kosher certifying organizations. Without changing the formula of many products, it's easy to tap the purchasing power of religious segments by obtaining this certification.

With a little effort and a great deal of vision, companies can capitalize on growth opportunities as never before in the vital, supersegmented consumer markets of America.

Bibliography

Books

Day, Carol Olsen, and Edmund Day. *The New Immigrants*. New York: Franklin Watts, 1985.

Greenberg, Eric et al. *Successful Marketing to U.S. Hispanics and Asians.* American Management Association Research Report. New York: AMACOM, 1987.

Kim, H. Edward. *Facts About Korea*. Seoul: Heron International, 1986.

Lepthien, Emilie. *Philippines*. Chicago: Children's Press, 1984.

Low, W. Agustus, and Virgil A. Clift. *Encyclopedia of Black Americans*. New York: Da Capo, 1981.

Melendy, H. Brett. *Asians in America: Filipinos, Koreans and East Indians*. Boston: Twayne, 1977.

O'Brien, David J., and Stephen S. Fugita. *The Japanese American Experience*. Bloomington and Indianapolis: University of Indiana Press, 1991.

Pascoe, Elaine. *Racial Prejudice: Issues in American History*. New York: Franklin Watts, 1985.

Rossman, Marlene L. *The International Businesswoman of the 1990s*. New York: Praeger, 1990.

Smead, Howard. *The Afro-Americans*. New York: Chelsea House, 1989.

Sowell, Thomas. *Ethnic America*. New York: Basic Books, 1981.

Steele, Shelby. *The Content of Our Character*. New York: St. Martin's Press, 1990.

Periodicals

American Demographics
Black Enterprise
Business Week
Ebony
Essence
Far Eastern Economic Review
Forbes
Fortune
Hispanic Business
Hispanic
Marketing News (American Marketing Association)
Newsweek
Sales and Marketing Management
The New York Times
The Wall Street Journal
Time
Transpacific
Village Voice

Index